What is Worth Teaching?

What is Worth Teaching?

Fifth edition

KRISHNA KUMAR

Orient BlackSwan

WHAT IS WORTH TEACHING?

ORIENT BLACKSWAN PRIVATE LIMITED

Registered Office
3-6-752 Himayatnagar, Hyderabad 500 029, Telangana, India
Email: centraloffice@orientblackswan.com

Other Offices
Bengaluru, Chennai, Guwahati, Hyderabad,
Kolkata, Mumbai, New Delhi, Noida, Patna

First published 1992
Second edition 1997
Third edition 2004
Fourth edition 2009
Fifth edition 2025

041934

ISBN 978-93-5442-637-7

Typeset in Adobe Garamond Pro 12/14.5 *by*
Shine Graphics, Delhi 110 094

Printed at
Kensington Printing & Packaging, Noida 201 301

Published by
Orient Blackswan Private Limited
3-6-752, Himayatnagar, Hyderabad 500 029, Telangana, India
Email: info@orientblackswan.com

Contents

Preface to the Fifth Edition

When *What is Worth Teaching?* was first published, nobody thought it would stay in the market for so long. It was much later that I realised that the secret to its long life lay in its title. The first edition was a thin little booklet, containing the text of three lectures. These I had delivered in the mid-1980s under the auspices of the University Grants Commission's 'national lectures' scheme. Professor Sureshchandra Shukla had nominated me for this scheme. The lectures were delivered at Baroda, Indore and Saugar. Each one had a history of its own gestation. Professor M.S. Yadav of Baroda saw great potential in the first of the three lectures. It had already been delivered once in Delhi at a seminar organized by Vinod Raina at the Nehru Memorial Museum and Library. He wanted me to speak about the concept of learning. He was an activist and I was worried about disappointing him with a rehash of familiar theories of learning; I thought of focusing instead on teaching and its relationship with curriculum. This focus led me to the magical title that gave this book its long, regenerative life.

This short history of the original edition serves three purposes. First, it helps me to recall friends who are no more with us. Secondly, it underlines a key resource for reflection on education—that is, the difference between the perspectives that teaching, as distinguished from learning, offers. And thirdly, it allows me to tell the readers—especially the younger ones—of this new edition, how a small booklet grew fatter with each new appearance. With the passage of time, as concerns about teaching and the curriculum found new relevance and articulation, the scope of the original book expanded. The system of education also expanded, posing fresh issues for researchers, teachers and officers-in-charge to reflect on the direction and substance of their pursuits. This latest edition marks yet another growth point of the slim publication that had made its first appearance in the mid-1980s, in a very different climate of educational work. The lecture-essay added to this new edition is about technology and its dominance over educational discourses today. It was delivered in 2015 as the D.S. Kothari memorial lecture at University of Delhi.

A major decision I had to take for this edition concerned updating. Luckily, most of the chapters in *What is Worth Teaching?* dealt with ideas and, therefore, had no quantitative or statistical data. The chapter on elementary education presented the statistics that were valid in the 1990s. They changed when Sarva Shiksha Abhiyan succeeded in improving enrollment and retention rates. After the promulgation of the Right to Education Act, the landscape of elementary education began to change quite significantly. However, the progress could not be sustained through the changing political and policy climate. Then came COVID-19. It altered both the situation and the policy so radically that earlier priorities became obsolete as did statistics. School closure of the COVID years is now behind us, but reliable quantified estimates of the impact that the pandemic and the policies followed during its run are not available. Nor has the census due in 2021 been conducted yet. All this makes the necessity of statistical updating irrelevant. New readers of the book will do better if they focus on the theoretical orbit and the method of argument than on the statistics of the period.

As this edition goes to press, I can hardly avoid recognising the change that education-related research and writing have gone through over the long period during which the earlier editions of this book were published. The field is richer now and the voices that comprise it are more diverse. At the same time, the surrounding fields—sociology, psychology and history of education—look somewhat depleted, reflecting the losses that higher education has suffered. Some of these losses were inevitable, given the diminishing support for the social sciences in state-run universities. The newly risen sun of private universities has yet to treat educational inquiry as a serious domain, one worth cultivating. All luminous private universities have centres of 'public policy', but strangely enough, that term excludes education. Nor do these institutions, with rare exceptions, treat teacher education as a worthwhile orbit to invest in.

The teaching and training of teachers are convulsing under the heat and glare of the new technologies that threaten to replace full-time teachers, having already taken away some of their key roles and responsibilities. The weird coinage *artificial intelligence* has found a respectable place among debate-worthy topics. In this new ethos, the question posed by this book born in the last decade of the previous century seems destined to attract greater attention than its earlier editions did.

KRISHNA KUMAR

1

What is Worth Teaching?

In our country we usually do not think of curriculum as a 'problem'—in the sense that it involves imperfect choices and decisions made on the basis of defensible, and therefore, challengeable perceptions. We have an educational culture that is firmly entrenched in the rock of 'received' knowledge.[1] In such a culture, nobody asks why a certain body of information happens to be equated with education. The influential American curriculum theorist, Tyler, would have been happy to find, under our very different climate and historical circumstance, a large number of people who are used to accepting the validity of a particular structuring of educational knowledge.[2] Another matter that would have pleased him in India more than in his own country is the ease with which dissociation between curriculum and the child's immediate socio-cultural and physical milieu is accepted, and the zeal with which 'principles' for curriculum designing, teacher training, and so on, are demanded and applied.

My concern is not with principles but rather with the problem of curriculum. Inherent in this declaration is the assumption that there are no principles for developing a curriculum, nor can there be any. By challenging the well-established notion that there are certain time-honoured, proven rules capable of guiding us when we want to prepare a curriculum for the education of children, I wish to emphasise that there is no escape from reflecting on the conditions prevalent in society and culture, if we want to design defensible curriculum. To my mind, the problem of curriculum is related to our perception of what kind of society and people we are, and to our vision of the kind of society we want to be. By taking shelter in the 'received' perspective and the 'principles of curriculum development' that it offers, we merely shun our responsibility and allow ourselves to be governed by choices made long ago or elsewhere under very different circumstances.

The problem of curriculum is related to the first of three key questions to which most of educational research and reflection is addressed:

- What is worth teaching?
- How should it be taught?
- How are the opportunities for education distributed?

Although the three questions are independent and can be pursued individually, they are related to each other at a deeper level. Until we arrive at that level in a shared or collective inquiry into education, we can pursue the first question—what is worth teaching?—by itself. Whatever we determine to be worthy of being taught will be a proper candidate for inclusion in the curriculum. The obvious issue is how to determine 'worth'. What kind of value can we put upon different types of knowledge to distinguish between worthy and unworthy types with regard to their becoming the substance of education for children.

We can distinguish between two routes for solving the problem. The first consists of deciding the worth of what we want to teach in view of the learner's needs and abilities. The second consists of determining worth in terms of the intrinsic value of what we want to teach. I intend to chalk out both these routes, and then decide how satisfactory or otherwise they might prove in solving the problem of curriculum as I have defined it.

Route One: Learner's Viewpoint

It makes immediate sense to assess the worth of something we are about to give by taking into account the receiver's viewpoint. Education is something that adults want to give children, so what could be better than judging the worth of what we want to teach in terms of the children's own perception of it? The use of an analogy of choosing a gift is helpful here; when we give a gift, we often choose it by considering the receiver's personality, likes, and needs. Attractive though the analogy is, to apply it to education has obvious difficulties. One difficulty arises out of the fact that education is not for just one child. Hundreds, in fact millions, of children may be involved. So we will not get very far by considering the likes and needs of each child. Most likely, we will have to be content with a generalised understanding of children's personalities.

The second difficulty in applying the gift metaphor to education arises from the very nature of knowledge that we as adults might possess about children. As adults, we may be able to think, to some extent, on behalf of children, but we cannot totally submerge ourselves in the child's point of view. I may be charged with mystifying childhood, but I feel it is important to remember that the ability to look at things from the child's viewpoint is a special kind of ability. There is evidence which says that for adults to have this ability they may require a certain cultural context. In the West, such a context was created by the spread of Rousseau's reflections and ideas on individuality and freedom at the time when industrialisation increased the need for childcare and the possibility of child survival and health. A fortuitous combination of circumstances, covering both material and ideational resources, permitted the efflorescence of the bourgeois concept of childhood in Europe. Much of what we call the modern, progressive theory of education assumes a social acceptance and universal validity of this concept. But, even a moment's reflection on the world of real children—in the vast underclass of our society or in the insecure, post-cold war West —will suffice to tell us how limited the validity of that late eighteenth-century concept of childhood is and how short its life may eventually be.

The point is that although it is appropriate to determine the worth of what we want to teach in terms of the child's perspective, it may be extraordinarily difficult for us as adults to take the child's perspective in the matter we are considering.[3] Three reasons for this difficulty may be distinguished. First, children are interested in *all* kinds of things or can develop interest in just about any form of knowledge, depending on how it is presented to them. So what is worth teaching and what is not are not particularly relevant questions from the children's point of view. Second, children cannot be expected to articulate their view on the worth of something which is as abstract as knowledge. Put simply, as Donaldson does, 'the young child is not capable of deciding for himself what he should learn; he is quite simply too ignorant'.[4] At best, what children can be normally expected to articulate is liking or preference, and this brings us to the third reason, namely, the likings expressed by children keep changing, as they grow older. Therefore, the child's articulation of his or her own preferences cannot provide us with a reliable basis for making sustainable decisions about what we should teach them.

Going by the first route then, our best chance lies in agreeing to think *on behalf of* children rather than in trying to find out what they think. Now if we agree on this more modest possibility, we can soon identify one basic sense in which 'worth' can be determined; 'It is worth teaching something only if it can be learnt'. I am referring to 'worth' in the sense of being worthy of the bother of teaching. This is admittedly a rather pedestrian sense of worth, but nevertheless a useful one, for it can protect us from putting in a lot of wasteful effort of which we can find numerous examples today. The mismatch between what modern child psychology tells us about how children learn on the one hand, and the expectations embedded in school curricula on the other, is so sharp and violent in our country that it seems an exercise in redundancy to identify little examples. Indeed, the danger of giving single examples is that people in charge of curriculum planning might respond by acknowledging these as lapses and remove them, leaving the edifice of an unlearnable curriculum intact.

The example I will discuss here belongs to the early phase of school learning when the distinction between knowledge and skill is a hard one to make. Learning basic skills, such as reading, involves the translation of several discrete kinds of knowledge of the world, people, and language to construct a highly dynamic system of decoding graphic signs. Recent research in the pedagogy of reading tells us that the success of reading instruction depends on the encouragement given to children to use their prior knowledge of language (in its oral form) and the world to decode printed texts meaningfully.[5] In the light of this research, the alphabet-centred instruction given in Indian primary schools, and the lack of incentives for children to use their hypothesis-forming ability, discourage children's search for meaning. Repeated failure to make sense of what they are reading damages the self-concept of many children, leading them to drop out of school—a destiny to which many other factors may contribute.[6] Out of the children who do learn to read, many become mechanical readers, in the sense that they can scan a printed page but cannot associate the text with their own experiences. We will return to this problem in the fourth chapter. Here it should suffice to say that if reading were taught in a manner in which it could be effectively learnt, the enormous wastage characteristic of our primary education would be less. At present, only the exceptionally persistent or motivated children are able to relate to the text, that is, to read in a meaningful way. This example clearly belongs to the second of the three questions I had set, namely how something should be taught.

Psychology and pedagogy can help us organise and teach knowledge and skills in effective ways. This is a significant contribution towards solving the problem of curriculum, but one that can be appreciated only after a decision has been made about what is worth teaching in the first place. In other words, psychology or pedagogy cannot tell us whether reading is worth teaching in the first place, but only how and when it should be taught. Psychology can tell us even less about the validity of combining different kinds of knowledge or skills under one school subject.[7] The choice of knowledge and the manner of structuring it have to be determined on some other grounds. If we wished to decide whether it would be a good idea to introduce the oral heritage of folklore as a compulsory school subject at the primary stage, no amount of psychological or pedagogical awareness would help us make this decision. The decision has to do with our perception of the importance of folklore in our socio-cultural milieu and in our vision of the role of education in relation to this milieu. It requires reflection on our conscious choices, the socio-economic and political underpinnings of these choices, and ultimately on the implication of choosing folklore as a school subject for all children. Once the decision to teach folklore has been taken, we can refer to child psychology and pedagogy to determine how to break up folklore into learnable and enjoyable sequences and what kind of teaching would most suit this new subject.

Route Two: The Value of Knowledge

Let us turn to the second route which consists of examining the worth of what we want to teach in terms of its intrinsic value. The word 'intrinsic' is difficult to interpret, and it can land us in trouble if we are not careful. So far we have examined Route One which involved ascertaining the worth of knowledge from the child's perspective. Our brief inquiry revealed that beyond a point this route presents enormous difficulties where one can identify knowledge that *cannot* be learnt. Beyond this point, Route One has little help to offer. Route Two differs from this inquiry in that it does not refer to the child. What we are after in this route is the possibility of identifying something intrinsically valuable in the knowledge we want to impart—something that would qualify it to be in the curriculum under the only condition that it is learnable (i.e., the condition that Route One has taught us to respect for its usefulness).

On the face of it, the kind of inquiry we are making appears to be like the inquiry philosophers are known to make by asking: 'What is true-knowledge?' What they want to know in that question is: What is real knowledge as opposed to spurious knowledge? Supposing a philosopher could answer this question, would it be of use to us as teachers of children? Again, in a rather too obvious a sense one would say 'yes'. If someone could convincingly distinguish true from false knowledge, surely no one would like to teach false knowledge. The problem arises when we recognise that unlike philosophical inquiry, education is a mundane business. Philosophy is supposedly concerned with the pursuit of truth or true knowledge, whereas education is mostly concerned with people, particularly people as parents, their aspirations (collectively expressed by the institutions they support), and with the social reality that shapes these aspirations. Education deals with knowledge in a rather limited context, which is defined by the social reality of a particular period of history and locale. Mannheim, I believe, was right in pointing out that the aims of education could only be grasped historically, because they are shaped by history and therefore change from one period and society to the next.[8]

Despite its interest in 'truth', education deals not so much with true knowledge (even if such a thing could be ascertained and acknowledged by all) as with what is perceived as knowledge in a given social milieu. However much teachers, many of whom may be inspired by ideals of one kind or another, may want to train children to distinguish truth from falsehood, they can only do this within the context of what has been perceived and installed in the curricula as worthwhile knowledge. Crudely speaking, they are in schools to teach what *counts* as knowledge. And, what counts as knowledge is a reconstruction, based on the selection made under given social circumstances. Out of the total body of available knowledge only a part of it can be treated as worthy of being passed on to the next generation; the rest waits in appropriate archives for either oblivion or resurrection depending on circumstances. This is, of course, a generalisation, for we know that 'society' is hardly a unitary system in the matter we are dealing with. At some point we will have to treat this matter more carefully by considering how the composition of society, and the corresponding composition of the structure of educational opportunities, affect the choices reflected in what is taught in schools.

For the time being, though, the generalisation that school knowledge is a reconstruction, involving a selection of knowledge, should suffice for us. It can help us recognise the wide-ranging interaction involved in the process of reconstruction of knowledge. The interaction involves creation, codification, distribution and reception, and it takes place under the shaping influence of the economy, politics, and culture. What knowledge becomes available in schools for distribution has to do with the overall classification of knowledge and power in society. Schools supply persons whose knowledge and skills are appropriate for tasks generated by the economy and supported by politics and culture. Schools are able to supply such persons with the help of appropriate reconstruction of knowledge. The 'star warrior' (scientists working on the 'star wars' project) delineated by Broad is not a product of fortuitous circumstances.[9] He is an unmistakable product of America's hegemonic global politics, economy, and culture, just as a member of the Indian Civil Service in the early twentieth century was a product of colonial India. The role of the American and the Indian educational systems in producing these archetypes is fully examinable in terms of the reconstructions of knowledge that the two systems offer to their respective clienteles.

Operating under the influence of the economy, politics, and culture, the system of education sullies knowledge with associations of various kinds. Each association is like a watermark; it cannot be rubbed off, for the agencies that leave the mark are more powerful than, indeed beyond the control of, education. By studying educational systems in the context of social and economic history we can find several examples of such associations. Let me examine two of them, the first one relating to science. India's exposure to the West under colonial rule contextualised science within the dynamics of colonisation. Owing to its association with colonisation by a Western society, science became the target of xenophobia in many quarters of anti-colonial consciousness and struggle. Apathy to science, or worse still, suspicion of science and hostility towards it grew as part of the nationalist consciousness. Baran cites the opposite situation in Japan:

> its good luck in being spared the mass invasion of Western fortune hunters, soldiers, sailors, and 'civilizers' saved it also from the extremes of xenophobia which so markedly retarded the spread of Western science in other countries of Asia.[10]

To gain entry into the Indian school curriculum, science had a hard struggle, and even though it now has a secure place, it covers only a narrow spectrum of the activities permitted in the school. Basically, the culture of Indian schools remains hostile to science. If, for the sake of brevity, I describe the culture of science as that of touching, manipulating, personally observing, and making sense, then the culture of our schools could well be described as promoting the reverse by counterposing all these. Fear of science and all that it stands for continues to be embedded in our school culture and curriculum; why it is not openly expressed is simply because it would be considered politically incorrect.

Gandhi's proposal for 'basic education' offers another example of the influence of the sociology of knowledge on the school curriculum. An important aspect of his proposal was the introduction of local crafts and productive skills in the school. In functional terms, the idea was to relate the school to the processes of production in the local milieu, with the declared aim of making the school itself a productive institution. Gandhi thought that the elementary school could not possibly get very far in a poor society if it did not fulfil a substantial part of its own needs.[11] But, apart from this functional aspect (the practicality of which has been rightly debated), the proposal for basic education also had a symbolic aspect to which considerably less attention has been given. Symbolically, by proposing to introduce local crafts and production-related skills and knowledge in the school, Gandhi was proposing the allocation of a substantive place in the school curriculum to systems of knowledge developed by and associated with oppressed groups of Indian society, namely artisans, peasants, and cleaners. It was no less than a proposal for a revolution in the sociology of school knowledge. For centuries, the curriculum had confined itself to knowledge associated with dominant castes. Basic education was proposing a subtle plan to create room for knowledge associated with lower castes, including the lowest. In a truly 'basic' school, children were expected to clean toilets.[12] Effective implementation of basic education would have seriously disturbed the prevailing hierarchy of the different monopolies of knowledge in our caste society. In functioning basic schools—and they would have been common schools—the cultural capital of the upper castes would not have carried the stamp of exclusive validity as appropriate school knowledge.

The association between certain forms of knowledge and certain social groups is of importance to education because it characterises the very image of the educated person prevalent in a society in a particular phase of its history. As a result of this association, education becomes synonymous with certain areas of knowledge and certain other corresponding areas of ignorance. Let me use an example from my own daily life as an educated man, though not quite what is known as the 'Westernised' Indian, but sufficiently so to be incapable of using the indigenous names of months. My illiterate house-help uses the Indian calendar and has little knowledge of the Western calendar. We often have considerable difficulty in determining whether we have understood each other. As an uneducated person, she expects that I won't know the system she is used to; conversely, I as an educated person expect that she might know only the Indian system. Our ignorance of each other's calendar contributes to our identities as educated and uneducated persons.

It so happens, obviously because of the economic and political dynamics of our society, that ignorance of her system is an attribute of my image as an educated man. I am not supposed to know whether *Sawan* comes first or *Aghan*. On the contrary, her ignorance of the Western calendar is proof of her lack of education because knowledge of the Indian calendar is not one of the attributes of the educated Indian. She is from a lower-caste background while I am not. The kind of knowledge she has is associated in post-colonial India with the poor and the illiterate. Brahmin priests using the Indian calendar for specific rituals do not disturb this association, for in using the Indian calendar they are not acting in their capacity as modern educated persons, but in their capacity and from their status as Brahmin priests.

In every age, the educated man is defined differently, according to the associations that areas of knowledge and corresponding areas of ignorance have with different social groups. The pattern of dominance and distribution of the power to define roles play a significant part in determining the attributes which the educated person will be expected to possess. Thus, the problem of determining the worth of a form of knowledge, to a certain extent, arises out of the distribution of knowledge in society. The distribution of knowledge at a particular point of time may be itself an indicator of the distribution of the opportunities to be educated. For someone who wants to make a curriculum, the question is: 'Out of the prevailing forms of knowledge, which ones will I choose?' It is this latter question that we have been pursuing along Route Two, and we have found that the educational worth of a form of knowledge cannot be determined merely on the basis of some intrinsic characteristics of the knowledge in question. We have seen how important a role symbolic associations play in shaping the perception of knowledge in society.

Need and Character of Deliberation

On the basis of this inquiry along the two routes, I wish to argue that the problem of curriculum cannot be dealt with as an act of social engineering. It is an act of deliberation. In a society like ours where material capital and cultural capital associated with education are so unequally distributed, curriculum deliberation cannot escape conflict. How shall this conflict be resolved? Any genuine deliberation is based on the assumption that no voice will be silenced. If it were possible to silence a voice, the problem of finding expression for it in education would not arise. Indeed, the contrary is more important: that in a polity where no voice can be expressly silenced, education may offer a useful means to phase out certain voices or to make them inaudible. Dominant groups may use education, more specifically the curriculum, to see to it that voices other than their own are represented so inadequately, feebly, or distortedly, that they develop a negative appeal and gradually lend themselves to be phased out in curriculum deliberation. None of this needs to be a conscious process; it actually may be a quiet, civilised dynamic of dominance. Agreeing to perceive curriculum design as an act and product of deliberation, rather than a given, rational construct, is by itself a good preparation for enervating the dynamic by which dominance is perpetuated.

The failure of education to reach the oppressed groups in our society is directly related to this dynamic. It is easy to lay the blame for this failure on weak motivation among the poor, and on administrative inefficiency. These are the culprits whose faces we have grown accustomed to seeing smeared in educational debates. But the failure also offers us evidence of the inadequacy and narrowness of curriculum deliberation in our society. Curriculum designing in the school stage is the charge of the bureaucracy of education which includes the quasi-bureaucracy of the state-controlled institutions of pedagogical research and training. It has never been treated as an act of deliberation. Inquiry into the structures of knowledge embedded in the prevailing curriculum has never been on the agenda. The task of reorganising the structures of knowledge, and the related task of reorganising the perspective from which knowledge will be represented have not been perceived as important tasks.

Curriculum deliberation is a social dialogue. The wider its reach, the stronger its grasp of the social conditions in which education is to function. One major way to expand the reach of curriculum deliberation is to include teachers in it, and this is where the problem of curriculum encounters its greatest challenge in the culture of education in India. In this culture, teachers are subordinate functionaries. They are not expected to have a voice, only the skill to teach. What little curriculum deliberation does take place in the higher circles of educational machinery, remains extremely poor owing to the absence of the teacher's voice. But this is not a plea merely for the involvement of a greater number of people in curriculum deliberation. Numbers matter, but more important is the capacity of a deliberation to be sensitive to the dialogues going on in the wider society. Judging the differential importance of specific dialogues and determining the stance education ought to take towards a dialogue are difficult tasks, but shunning them would mean permitting the curriculum to remain aloof from the concerns of the wider society. This is the situation we are in and have been in for a long time.[13] Issues that common people are grappling with find no reflection or trace in the school's curriculum. The knowledge imparted in the classroom transcends all living concerns that children as members of society might have, as well as all other concerns that adult members of the powerless sections of the society have. A thin veneer of 'national' concerns, most of which are linked to the economically and culturally dominant groups, attempts to distract attention from the absence of issues facing the daily lives of ordinary men and women. This kind of transcendental curriculum is not just wasteful, for it does not use the opportunity that the school provides for imparting contextual knowledge; it is destructive too, for it promotes a kind of schizophrenia and domesticated consciousness. The educated man produced by a transcendental curriculum sees and seeks to establish no relation between his education and his personal life and conduct. A colonial educationist, Mayhew, had noted this feature of our education system sixty years ago:

> When the educated Indian is most himself, in the expression of his deepest emotion, and in the domestic or communal enjoyment of his leisure, he shows the least trace of what our schools and colleges have given him.[14]

Pedagogical planning, since Independence, has attempted to bypass rather than remedy the dissociation between our schools and our society. The name of the bypass was psychologism, which consists of the claim that the broad principles of child psychology are an adequate basis for developing suitable curricula and materials. We have seen earlier that psychology can at best provide a limited answer to the problem of curriculum. But one school of psychologism needs to be examined in special, for it has virtually ruled the minds of many of our avowedly modern and scientifically oriented institutions of pedagogical research and planning, particularly since the 1960s. The school I am referring to is that of 'behavioural objectives' of education schematised in a taxonomy by Bloom.[15] Followers of this school argue that the objectives of curriculum and teaching need only be defined in behaviour terms, such as 'analysing', 'translating', or 'inferring'. What knowledge content is used to achieve these behavioural aims is immaterial. The idea is to allow the child to develop skills that can be used in relation to any context or situation. This view of curriculum is often called the 'process model', for it emphasises the process of learning more than the content, i.e., how something is learnt rather than what is learnt. Clearly, the model denies the problem we have been discussing, namely the problem of identifying worthwhile knowledge in relation to the milieu, particularly the socio-cultural milieu of the child. It promises a technical means to transcend the milieu, and it legitimises such transcendence in the name of effective instruction. The model had obvious appeal for Indian educationists who had been accustomed, since the beginning of colonial policies in education, to seeing the socio-cultural milieu as an obstruction rather than an asset for education. The behavioural model came here during the 1960s, the so-called 'development decade', when Indian planners were eagerly looking towards the West, particularly towards America, to find technical solutions to all kinds of problems.

The promise of the behavioural brand of psychologism is a deceptive one, as Daniels has already shown and I will merely elaborate on Daniels's critique.[16] The fault lies in ignoring the nature of action concepts. Actions or behaviours (e.g., obeying, analysing, etc.) do not have a one-to-one relationship with certain acts. One act of obeying may be altogether different in its motivation, aim, and implications from another act of obeying, depending on the circumstances under which the act has to be performed. To use Daniels's term, action concepts are polymorphous in that they stand in a superordinate relationship to subordinate acts. Many different kinds of acts or behaviours can be accommodated under the label 'obeying' or 'analysing'; and these same acts can be classified under other action concepts. This is how labels such as 'loyalty', 'discipline', and 'service' came so handy to educational planners of Hitler's Germany. By merely using behavioural labels to characterise the intended curriculum, we do not solve the basic problem of curriculum formulation, but evade it at an enormous risk of distortion of the aims of education that we may have in mind. Only by examining the intentions of the learner, the conditions under which learning has to occur, and the means of teaching to be used can we recognise what precisely will happen.

This is how the problem of curriculum is related to the distribution of education opportunities and to methods of teaching. The distribution of opportunities for learning available in a society is an important factor that influences both how 'worth' of a certain kind of knowledge is perceived or weighed and how knowledge that is regarded as worthy of being taught will be represented in educational materials. We can take for granted that the knowledge relevant or related to groups whose access to education is poor will not be regarded as worthy of being taught in schools. Who would regard, for example, the knowledge of the Baiga myth of the world's creation as worthwhile educational knowledge? For that matter, even the knowledge of animal behaviour and medicinal plants that the Baiga have acquired over a lengthy acquaintance with the jungles of central India is unlikely to be regarded as worthwhile educational knowledge. The possibility of including the Baiga experience in the curriculum depends on the Baiga's own access to education and their performance in today's competitive ethos. Baiga children have poor access to opportunities for education and their chances of doing well at school are very slim, at least partly because the Baiga's life finds no resonance in the school curriculum.[17] The school is the outpost of an alien culture and system of knowledge in a Baiga village.

How the method of teaching affects the character of what is taught can be seen in the teaching of science. The distinctness of science as a school subject comes from the need for experimentation by the learner. Of course it is possible to teach science without experimentation, but then it loses its distinctness from subjects like literature and history. If distinctness is a criterion for considering an area of knowledge as a separate school subject, then there is no point in teaching science without providing the opportunity to experiment. As a subject that demands experimentation and independent inquiry by the learner, science is associated with freedom of judgement and equality between the student and the teacher in the presence of objective facts. Science education is supposed to be conducive to secular values precisely because it makes ascribed authority redundant. But if science is taught in a traditional manner, with the authority of the textbook and the teacher's word, and without opportunity for experimentation, it would cease to have a secular character and value. Once it loses its original character, owing to the application of conventional pedagogies, science can easily become an instrument for authoritarian control in the classroom and in society. The practice of science in a milieu that does not permit equality or open questioning might lead pupils into imbibing values that are antithetical to science. Also, science can reinforce existing structures of dominance if its content and the method of teaching are not reorganised from the perspective of powerless social groups.

And, not just the character of what is taught, but the volume of content, too, is affected by the methods of teaching. For some time now, a favourite theme among curriculum developers in India has been the 'load' or volume of content described in the syllabus for each class. No solution is likely to be found for the problem of 'curriculum load' until it is diagnosed correctly. The problem of volume of content at any grade level does *not* originate in the so-called 'explosion of knowledge' which is frequently referred to in our country in discussions of curriculum. It originates in the archaic notion of curriculum as a bag of facts and in the equally archaic view of teaching as a successful delivery of known facts. Unless we shed these notions and take a more dynamic view of curriculum and teaching, we are going to remain stuck with impossibly large syllabi and fat and dry textbooks. The quasi-bureaucratic organisations responsible for curriculum planning in our country will go on packing the syllabi tighter and tighter, all the time seeking justification in the explosion of knowledge with which our 'backward' country will have to cope. This process of mistaken action and legitimation of action can stop only if we recognise that curriculum planning involves a selection of knowledge, and teaching involves the process of creating a classroom ethos in which children *want* to pursue inquiry. We hardly need to add that a curriculum based on this view of teaching can be prepared and implemented only *after* the teacher's right to participate in the organisation of knowledge and the child's right to autonomy in learning are accepted.

During the early 1990s, the central government appointed a committee to make an inquiry into the problem of curriculum load and to recommend ways to remedy it. Popularly known as the Yashpal committee, it located the root of the problem of curriculum load in the concept of knowledge that pervades the system.[18] This concept, the Yashpal report says, dissociates the processes of learning and teaching from the construction or production of knowledge. Learning gets reified when it is perceived in terms of regurgitable information to be acquired. Such a limited viw of learning is partly derived from colonial assumptions regarding who the producers and the consumers of knowledge are. This is how the Yashpal report interpreted the popular idea that there has been an explosion of knowledge in the twentieth century, and the related idea that in order to cope with this explosion, a country like India must teach a vast body of knowledge during the early school years. The report debunked this kind of of teaching in fairly direct terms. Both the analysis and the recommendations presented by the Yashpal committee were widely discussed and appreciated—the parliament also approved it—but no substantial change in curricular policies or textbook writing took place. The controversial National Curriculum Framework, 2000, turned the Yashpal discourse into rhetoric and used the complaint of curriculum load as an excuse for making ideologically inspired changes in textbooks, particularly in the social sciences. The new textbooks of history and other subjects produced by the NCERT in 2002 give ample evidence to show that the analysis presented in the Yashpal report proved too subtle for the system to absorb. Whether the system can be reformed in isolation from the larger social ethos was a point Professor Yashpal had himself made in his letter to the minister. The ethos of the early years of the new century presents a far grosser set of challenges to the system of education than what it has faced at any point in its history. A major political enterprise to transform the basic character of the Indian republic seems to have also encircled education, at least for now. The gloomy state of mind in which reform-seekers in education find themselves once again reminds us how important it is to view the school curriculum as an exercise of wide-ranging deliberation in society.

Notes

1. For the distinction between the 'received' and the 'dynamic' perspective on curriculum, see John Eggleston, *The Sociology of the Curriculum* (London: RKP, 1977). Basically, the 'received' perspective is derived from an *apriori* view of knowledge, whereas the 'dynamic' perspective—the one used in this paper—places knowledge in a sociological context and inquires into its legitimacy.
2. Ralph Tyler's *Basic Principles of Curriculum and Instruction* (Chicago: University of Chicago Press, 1950) has had an influence worldwide, and it is not unusual to come across postgraduate students and professors of education in India who, to this day, quote Tyler's definition of education, without attributing it to him. The

definition, which squarely places education and curriculum in the domain of psychology, is that education is a process of changing the behaviour patterns of people. The emphasis Tyler placed on behaviour was furthered in the *Taxonomy of Educational Objectives* (New York: David McKay, 1956) prepared by Benjamin Bloom and his colleagues. It continues to be referred to in India and has been recently reborn in the term 'minimum levels of learning'.

3. The difficulty does not, of course, prevent the use of the term 'child-centred' as a cliche to legitimise some new programme or material. Like many other terms used in political and development discourse, 'child-centred education' has been imported from Europe and is now freely used in India without the least reference to or worry about the material and cultural conditions under which it emerged in Europe.
4. Margaret Donaldson, *Children's Minds* (London: Fontana, 1978).
5. Much of the recent work on reading is based on the application of a psycholinguistic perspective. It is interesting that the insights which this perspective has provided are consistent with the conclusions reached independently by people such as Sylvia Ashton-Warner and Bruno Bettelheim through their own experiences.
6. For understandable reasons, this cause is seldom cited in drop-out research. For a reconstruction of how this process might occur in the life of a child, see my 'Ashok ki Kahani', *Itwari Patrika* (25 May 1986).
7. Consider, for example, the combination of history, geography, and civics under 'social studies'. This combination acquires its legitimacy from the modern understanding of the social sciences, but the construction of knowledge taught in civics in Indian schools is based neither on child psychology nor social science, but rather on the colonial perception of the native. For a discussion of the development of the civics curriculum under colonial rule, see Arthur Mayhew, *The Education of India* (London: Faber, 1926).
8. Karl Mannheim and W.A.C. Stewart, *An Introduction to the Sociology of Education* (London: RKP, 1962).
9. Philip G. Altbach in a review of *Star Warriors* by W.J. Broad, *Economic and Political Weekly*, 31 (26 July 1986): 30, says: 'Broad's scientific warriors are your typical computer nerds found on any

college campus. They are brilliant scientists trained at the best schools in the country such as MIT and Cal Tech, but they have little sense of politics and little education beyond physics, computer science and other technological areas. They live in a self-contained universe of top-secret clearance, high-level science and a feeling that somehow it is all a technological game that can supply America with a technological "fix" that can protect us from the Russians.' The 'star warriors' studied by Broad are the scientists who are actually involved in a star wars programme.

10. P.A. Baran, *The Political Economy of Growth* (New York: Monthly Review Press, 1957) 160.
11. See T.S. Avinashilingam's *Gandhiji's Experiments in Education* (Delhi: Ministry of Education, 1960).
12. See Marjorie Sykes, *New Schools in Bihar* (Patna: Bihar Government Press, 1948).
13. How this situation is reified in the 'textbook culture' that dominates the Indian education system is discussed in the next chapter.
14. Mayhew, op cit, 207.
15. The National Council of Educational Research and Training (NCERT) was established in the early 1960s. Many of its pedagogues were trained in the United States at the time when Bloom's behavioural objectives (see note 2) were extremely popular there.
16. L.B. Daniels, 'What is the Language of the Practical?' *Curriculum Inquiry Network* 4 (4: 1975): 61, 237.
17. For a study and discussion of the situation in which a tribal student is placed when confronted by a lesson that denies or distorts his worldview, see my *Social Character of Learning* (New Delhi: Sage, 1989).
18. *Learning Without Burden* (New Delhi: NCERT, 1993).

2

Origins of the Textbook Culture

Textbooks are universally used but they mean different things in different countries. Their practical use in the school's daily routine and their symbolic function varies from one educational system to the next. In some countries, textbooks are published only by private publishers; in others, only by the government. In certain countries, state authorities merely recommend suitable textbooks, leaving school authorities and teachers free to select the ones they like; in others, specific textbooks are prescribed by the state, and no deviation is expected or allowed. In some countries, textbooks are purchased by the school and provided to children; in others, children must buy their own copies of the prescribed textbooks and carry them to school every morning in capacious schoolbags.

Perhaps the most important variation, from the viewpoint of pedagogy and curriculum, is in the manner in which textbooks are used. In some educational systems, the teacher decides when she wants children to consult a textbook. She prepares her own curricular plan and mode of assessment, and she decides which materials, printed or otherwise, she wants to use. Textbooks are just one of the many aids available to her. Such freedom can only be dreamt of in other educational systems where the teacher is tied to the prescribed textbook. She has no choice—in curriculum, or materials, or assessment. A textbook is prescribed for each subject, and the teacher has to teach it, lesson by lesson, until there are no more lessons left. She must ensure that the children can do the exercises given at the end of each lesson without help, for this is what they will have to do in the final examination. The textbook symbolises the authority under which the teacher must accept to work. It also symbolises the teacher's subservient status in the educational culture.

Since, the use of textbooks, the process of their production, and their symbolic function in the teacher's daily routine varies so much, it is wrong to talk of textbooks in a global sense. Yet, that is what happens all the time. Pedagogical writings typically assume that textbooks have a universally accepted function. And, it is not just pedagogical writings, even educational-planning exercises are often based on the assumption that textbooks are a value-free, globally relevant input. International studies and aid-based production of textbooks are often based on such an assumption. Yet, it ought to be self-evident that when the World Bank finances a project to improve textbooks in the Philippines, or when a Canadian publisher modifies a textbook to make it marketable in the West Indies, or when a team of textbook writers in an Indian organisation at the state level consults an American textbook to gain new ideas—in each case, the term 'textbook' refers to a distinct commodity whose practical and symbolic functions will be shaped by the socio-economic and cultural milieu in which it will be used. In each case, the textbook will be a part of the overall educational culture whose meanings will be determined by the structures of interaction prevailing among state authorities, teachers, and children.

In the ordinary Indian school, the textbook dominates the curriculum. The teacher is bound by the textbook since it is prescribed, and not just recommended, by state authorities. Each child must possess his own copy of the textbook prescribed for each subject, and he must carry all the textbooks along with notebooks (popularly called 'copies') to school every day. The teacher spends most of the time in class simplifying or interpreting the textbook and familiarising students with its content to the point where it can be easily memorised. With some variation in different subjects and at different levels, the textbook is used for class routines such as loud reading, silent reading, comprehension exercises, recapitulation, homework, and tests. At all levels of school education, the textbook acts as a substitute syllabus or rather as the operative part of the syllabus. Students expect to be examined strictly within the limits of what the textbook contains on any topic. For the teacher, it acts as a structuring device, offering a programme of sequenced action which applies uniformly to all schools within a provincial or nation-wide system.

Colonial Roots

The argument that I wish to present here is that the textbook-centred character of school pedagogy in India is related to the historical circumstances under which India's present education system developed. More specifically, the roots of the textbook culture can be traced to the early nineteenth century when the East India Company took certain definite steps for establishing an education system. The new system acquired a final, bureaucratic format in 1854 from Sir Charles Wood's Despatch. Among the major decisions taken by the colonial administrator during this period, the following are of special interest to us:

1. The new system would be governed by a bureaucracy at every stage from primary schooling onwards, and in all aspects including the structure of syllabi, the content of textbooks, and teacher training;

2. the new system would aim at acculturating Indian children and youth in European attitudes and perceptions, and at imparting to them the skills required for working in colonial administration, particularly at its middle and lower rungs;
3. the teaching of English and its use as a medium of instruction would be a means of this acculturation and training;
4. indigenous schools would have to conform to the syllabus and textbooks prescribed by the colonial government if they wanted to seek government aid;
5. impersonal, centralised examinations would be used to assess students' eligibility for promotion and to select candidates for scholarships.

The textbook culture originated in the operational meaning that these policies acquired under the socio-economic and cultural conditions prevailing in India at the time. These conditions are not easy to characterise. The procedures applied by the coloniser to gain control of the indigenous economy, and later the indigenous culture, became increasingly complex as the Indian response to colonisation developed contradictions originating in class interests and cultural instincts. In general, even as the native economy, with its subsistence agriculture and village-based crafts, crumbled under the pressure of taxation and foreign goods, new aspirations surfaced among the class of people who had profited by acting as middlemen between the English colonisers and the Indian populations.[1] These aspirations acted as catalysts for the reception of the colonisers' worldview through education. Colonial education meant that its beneficiaries would begin to perceive themselves and their society as consumers of the knowledge supplied by the coloniser, and would cease to see themselves as people capable of producing new knowledge.[2]

Education was thus supposed to reinforce culturally what colonial policies were aimed at achieving economically. Colonial economic policies in India were aimed at creating a class of consumers of goods manufactured in the coloniser's home country. Steps taken for upliftment of the colony were not meant to establish a production economy (for this would have harmed the very purpose of establishing a colony in the first place), but rather to legitimise and consolidate administrative control. Colonial policies did not leave just the productive capacities of the Indian society untouched, they actually destroyed such capacities through direct means like introduction of new land systems and the dumping of British machine-made goods, and indirect means like education involving training in unproductive skills and socialisation in colonial perceptions.[3]

Teachers and Teaching

The imposition of a bureaucratically controlled system of education had a dramatic impact on the old vocation of teaching. Instruction in basic skills was widespread in many parts of India at the time that colonial control of the economy was established. Religious schools were also common. Teaching as a vocation had a base in the caste structure, and had been known in the subcontinent for many centuries as a special form of social activity. Teachers had traditionally enjoyed reverence. Often, they combined priestly functions with teaching. In the indigenous schools surveyed by Adam in 1835, the teacher exercised autonomy in choosing what was worth teaching and in deciding how to teach it. The curriculum mostly consisted of an acquaintance with culturally significant texts, and the learning of skills useful to the village society.[4] In these matters, most teachers went by conventions, but they had the freedom to make choices.

The new system of centralised official control eroded the teacher's autonomy by denying him any initiative in matters pertaining to the curriculum. Not that the earlier situation offered many alternatives, but it did not impose choices as the new system did. Apart from the official curriculum and texts, the new system also imposed on the teacher the responsibility to fulfil official routines, such as maintenance of admission registers, daily diaries, record of expenditure, and test results. These routine activities were affected by the fear of punishment and monetary cuts, particularly when student performance during inspections began to be used as a criterion for financial grants. The fear led not just to sycophancy and self-debasement, as in the zealous waving of English flags at the time of inspection, but even to the tendency to give extra punishment in case there was any suspicion that a boy might have offended the inspecting officer.[5]

The teachers' attitude towards bureaucratic authority, and their acceptance of sticking to the prescribed textbook, can hardly be understood properly without taking into account the enormous difference of salary and status between the teacher and the officer.[6] At the beginning of the century, a primary school teacher's salary was ten times less than the salary of a Provincial Education Service officer, and at least four times less than that of a Subordinate Education Service officer. In 1920, when a trained primary school teacher in the United Provinces had to start his career with Rs 17 a month, a deputy inspector started at Rs 170, and a sub-deputy inspector at Rs 70. In Bombay, where teachers got a somewhat higher start, a trained primary teacher was given about Rs 30 while the average for an officer of the Provincial Education Service was Rs 486 and that for an officer of the Subordinate Education Service, Rs 114 per month. Along with this striking difference in salaries went the contrast in power and status. A sub-deputy inspector could mar a teacher's career and therefore inspired awe.

Among the new professions that emerged with the consolidation of colonial rule after the 1857 revolt, such as legal and medical practice, teaching soon acquired a low position. Compared to the civil service, school teaching meant a socially powerless, low-paid job, and compared to other professions such as law and medicine, teaching projected a rather unspecialised image. A substantial part of a school teacher's daily routine consisted of fulfilling official requirements such as the maintenance of accurate records of admission, tests, and money. For a long time, maintaining a carefully recorded stock of prescribed textbooks and dispensing them for a small commission was among the official responsibilities of the teacher in several parts of British India.[7]

Had the teachers been given a role in syllabus preparation, and had they been given the freedom to choose suitable textbooks, their identity could perhaps have competed better with that of other professions which offered autonomy in professional matters. The possibility of such autonomy being granted to the teachers could only have arisen out of a demand made by them, or as a result of reform in the policies of the education department. Poor salary and status kept the first route blocked, and the other was obstructed by vested interests. Such interests did not exist when textbook production first started under the auspices of a School Book Society in Calcutta in 1817. But as soon as schooling facilities expanded, particularly after the mid-nineteenth century, vested interests developed rapidly.

A letter in *The Statesman* in 1868 complained that 'every inspector has his own friends and prestiges to serve, and thus a good deal of jobbery is perpetrated in the name of uniformity in textbooks.'[8] Missionary houses were among the dominant interests in the textbook business, and as the century advanced they were joined by houses importing or reprinting books published in England. Three major English firms, namely Oxford University Press, Macmillan, and Longmans, established offices in India in the early years of the twentieth century. The influence they carried in curriculum committees, consisting mainly of bureaucrats, was far stronger than what Indian publishing houses could muster.[9] This situation changed a little after Indian ministers were appointed in the education department in the wake of administrative reforms in 1921. The average teacher's lack of freedom to choose textbooks remained unchanged. His role continued to be confined to helping children learn, or rather learn by heart, whatever text had been prescribed by the department's bureaucracy.

The textbook culture was a product of both archaic pedagogical practices as it existed and conditions created by the colonial bureaucracy. The pedagogical practices regarded memorising as a mode of academic achievement. This is how W.D. Arnold, the director of Public Instruction in Punjab during 1857–58, described the concept of learning that he found popular among the people of Punjab:

> We found a whole population agreed together that to read fluently and if possible to say by heart a series of Persian works of which the meaning was not understood by the vast majority, and of which the meaning when understood was for the most part little calculated to edify the minority, constituted education.[10]

The new textbooks could not change the existing convention of mechanical reading and rote learning. Rather, the convention found in the new textbooks a convenient agency to perpetuate itself. If only the new education had tried to relate learning to the child's real life and milieu it would have posed a threat to the existing convention of learning. This could have happened if teachers had received a better deal, both in terms of money and status, at the hands of bureaucrats. The colonial administration chose not to increase its financial burden by increasing teachers' salaries. It left the teacher in a meek professional role which could only perpetuate a textbook culture.

Examinations and the Curriculum

The policy of impersonal, centralised examinations made a major contribution to the textbook culture. Examinations were impersonal in the sense that students were examined by someone other than the teacher. The idea of impartial assessment meant on the spot testing by the inspecting official, and public, written examinations at the end of the course. In these examinations, secrecy had to be maintained over both the question papers and the identity of the examiners. With its aura of strictness and impartial treatment of all examinees, the examination system played an important role in the development of a bureaucratic system of education. To the English administrator, examinations, like textbooks, were a means of norm-maintenance. As Shukla has pointed out, colonial policy used written examinations to evolve a bureaucratic, centralised governance of education.[11] The official function of the examination system was to evolve uniform standards for promotion, scholarship, and employment, and thereby to consolidate government control. In the social context, the examination system served the purpose of instilling in the public mind the faith that colonial rule was fair and free of prejudice. It imparted this faith by being impersonal, hence non-discriminatory in appearance, and by being so wrapped up in secrecy.

In practical terms, the examination system required students to rehearse endlessly the skills of reproduction from memory, summarising, and essay-type writing on any topic. Students were examined on their study of specific texts, not on their understanding of concepts or problems. An early report by Kerr records that when the first uniform code of rules was prepared for government institutions in Bengal, the 'class-books' on which candidates were to be examined for scholarships were specified.[12] A little later, in 1845, an even greater narrowing of the syllabus was implemented by 'fixing' not just the particular textbooks but 'the exact portion' from each book to be studied for the next scholarship examination.

Whatever could not be examined within the norms of the examination system (i.e., a written, essay-type answer to be assessed by an examiner unknown to the student) was kept out of the curriculum, however useful, relevant, and interesting it might have been. This is how theoretical, especially literary, study acquired a dominant place in Indian schools and colleges. Literary study fitted nicely within the frame of the textbook culture and written examinations. Practical or vocational skills, and subjects dependent on practical skills, such as science subjects, were a misfit in the frame. For a long time they were not allowed a place in the approved curriculum, and later on when they were allowed a place, it was peripheral. Literature had an advantage over science as it was perceived in the formative phase of colonial policy as a useful instrument of acculturation. As Chatterjee has mentioned, an important difference between the view of J.S. Mill and Macaulay, both influential theoreticians of the early nineteenth-century colonial policies, was that Mill considered both European literature and science necessary for the education of Indian children whereas Macaulay favoured only literature.[13] It was Macaulay's view which prevailed even though Mill's position had its supporters among influential Indians like Raja Rammohan Roy. Emphasis on literary study set the stage for textbook culture, and once the textbook culture was born, it reinforced the dominance of literary study and skills in the curriculum.

Another implication of the examination-textbook link was that the curriculum remained alien, even hostile, to the student's milieu. Since examination was centralised, it could only accommodate the most general kinds of information as opposed to information reflecting a specific milieu. In a country like India, where local milieus are so sharply varied, both geographically and culturally, the demands of a centralised examination system could only be met by a curriculum that transcended local or regional specificity. The nature of questions appropriate for essay-type answers complemented this tendency of the curriculum. The tendency was further strengthened by the dominant role that colonial perceptions played in the selection and representation of knowledge. At the height of the Victorian period, the colonial perception of India consisted of broad impressions of the degeneracy of her culture and the destructive effects of her climate on the Indian character. As Welsh has shown, these impressions were reflected in school and college textbooks.[14] The sweeping nature of such impressions—which were both products and feeders of the Victorian tendency to form grand theories about why certain races were backward and certain others so far ahead—found a fitting medium in the textbooks prepared for a centralised examination system. At another level, only this kind of generalised 'knowledge' could be expected to fulfil the agenda of acculturating the Indian student in colonial perceptions and attitudes. Any specific or locally relevant knowledge of social affairs, politics, or even one's own life and surrounding was debarred.

A more specific case of how alienation of the curriculum strengthened the textbook-examination linkage and the textbook culture can be found in English as a school subject. The textbook written for the teaching of English use literary pieces whose idiom and images were mostly steeped either in the domestic world of the Victorian bourgeois, or in its counterpoint —the natural world of Wordsworth and his early contemporaries. Neither of the two worlds was accessible to the Indian student.

Poems about the English spring or winter were as unrelated and strange to the Indian climate as were the happy-family stories foreign to the Indian way of life. Texts of this kind could *not* be read for meaning: they could only be memorised. Conventional pedagogy of reading, too, contributed to the tendency to memorise, but the role of alien symbolism in making the texts unintelligible was equally significant. Lester gives a useful description of how textbook literature encouraged the tendency to memorise lessons for reproduction at the examination:[15]

> Stories in one-syllabled words that English children enjoy, tales of domestic life, of cats, of faithful dogs, of snow and skating, only muddled the minds of those who had never seen ice nor felt cold, who were trained never to let a dog, which ate filth, come near them. As for the pictures which accompany two syllable-worded stories about kettles and tea-pots, pudding and turkeys and cosy fireplaces in the cottage kitchens where a table is spread for Sünday dinner, and chairs are drawn up while everyone bows the head to listen to the father asking the blessing, it seemed a mad, if not immoral, world that was being presented. The only thing to do was to learn it all by heart and repeat it rapidly when called upon.

The precise effect of the examination system on the student's orientation towards education cannot be understood without taking into account the relationship between examinations and the opportunities for education and employment. The examination system served as a turnstile between the opportunities for education and the opportunities for employment. Although the educational opportunities, in relation to the population, remained very limited throughout the colonial period, they outnumbered the opportunities for employment shortly after the new system of education was introduced. The colonial rule was not designed to, and never did, release the productive energies of the Indian society; the only opportunities for work that it could create were in the administrative domain. By the last quarter of the nineteenth century, this domain was already saturated. Despite the extremely narrow spread of education, people with certificates and degrees could not be accommodated in government jobs any more. Examinations were now required to play a far wider role than that of norm-maintenance within the education system. The new role was to keep eligibility for jobs under severe control by keeping the rate of failure high. Any lowering of this rate led to immediate worry among the colonial rulers.[16] The matriculate and the B.A. examinations, in particular, became carefully guarded turnstiles to keep the numbers of those going across them under strict control. Loosening the turnstile would be an invitation for social discontent arising out of unemployment of the eligible.

This function of examinations as an agency of social control resulted in a deep fear of failure among young people. The fear became part of the lore of childhood, and the consequences of failure became a recurring motif in literature.[17] The fear of failure in the examination had repercussions both on classroom interaction and students' own strategies of preparation. When the main concern of both the teacher and student was to prevent failure at the examination, the best possible use of classroom teaching could only be to prepare students as meticulously as possible for the examination and this was done by confining teaching to the contents of the prescribed textbook. On the student's side, the ability to commit vast amounts of printed text to memory became highly valuable. Storage of knowledge for guaranteed reproduction in the examination at the end of the year would hardly have been possible without the construction of a strong symbolic association between knowledge and the prescribed textbooks. Metaphors of bodily storage of knowledge became a part of children's culture. In the biographical account of his Punjabi ancestry from the middle of the nineteenth century, Prakash Tandon recalls how in his grandfather's days,[18]

> the boys had coined a Punjabi expression, remembered even in our day, wishing that they could grind the texts into a pulp and extract knowledge out of them and drink it.

The examination-textbook linkage became stronger as the system of education expanded and as the stagnation of work opportunities exacerbated the competitive character of the system. The linkage defeated all attempts to reform the curriculum and the methods of teaching. Gradually, this defeat utterly diluted the spirit with which ideas and programmes of reform were voiced and heard. Commission after commission, starting with the Hunter Commission of 1882–83, bemoaned the stultifying role that examinations had begun to play. Similarly, the obsolete nature of the curriculum was criticised and exhortations were made to change it. Writing in 1910, Alston drew attention to his feeling that colleges had become rival cramming institutions, and pointed out how absurd it was that politics, history, and economics were taught from single texts.[19] 'Books and not subjects are prescribed', he wrote, expressing his impatience with the narrowness of the curriculum and with the tendency among both students and teachers to identify the curriculum with the textbooks. Alston's irritation over the absurdity of the situation and the impossibility of reform is just one sample of what was to become the perpetual mood of educational discourse in India.

Finally, the use of English as a compulsory subject in the secondary school, and as a medium of instruction and examination, could well be assigned an important role in the rise and perpetuation of the textbook culture. As a foreign language, English posed a dual challenge to the Indian student. He was first supposed to master its grammar and basic vocabulary, and then use this barely mastered medium for the study of other school subjects. English was not a part of the average student's ethos, nor could the average student ever hope to be exposed to a native speaker of English. Learning the language meant making the best use of the dictionary, the textbooks (especially the textbook for grammar), and classroom instruction which was devoted to the teaching of the textbooks and grammar. The famous Bengali scientist, P.C. Ray, described the place English held in the curriculum in 1913:[20]

> A boy in an ordinary school from IV onward has to learn something of grammar, composition, phrases, idioms, homonyms, synonyms, difference between 'shall' and 'will', etc. Now for the matriculation course over and above these, he is expected to have mastered the contents of at least a dozen standard books. Even on taking up his I.S.C. course, he is not exempted from the overwhelming burden of textbooks of English Prose and Poetry.

Learning English under such circumstances could only mean an enormous and continuous effort, on a scale that would leave no time or energy to grapple with the subject matter of other school disciplines. Memorisation of the textbooks of these other subjects was the only convenient way to avoid failure at the examination. As Annie Besant explained, the students were struggling to follow the language while they should have been grasping the facts. Their only resource was to utilise their extraordinary power of memorising by learning textbooks by heart and reproducing them in the examination.[21]

After Independence

Structures of pedagogical transaction, once established, do not give in to change easily. Colonial pedagogy outlasted colonial rule—in independent India, curriculum continues to be textbook bound. While the system of education has expanded enormously since Independence, it has not been able to shed colonial policies of examinations and the prescription of textbooks. A major change has come in textbooks production with the emergence, mainly since the sixties, of state corporations which have monopoly rights over the publication of textbooks, especially for the elementary grades. The state has thus extended its role well beyond that of choosing suitable texts and prescribing them. The establishment of the NCERT in the early sixties further reified the state's responsibility in curriculum and textbooks by creating a permanent organisational base for these matters. Private publishers still have some interest in the business of school textbooks, but their clientele is restricted mainly to private, especially unaided schools.

Teacher training and examinations continue to be two 'weak' areas of the system. Since school teaching has continued to be a low-status profession, teacher training remains a poorly rated academic field. The training of elementary-level teachers in particular, and all school teachers in general, remains largely untouched by an academic grounding in modern child-centred pedagogy. Such grounding might possibly dilute the patterns of teacher-pupil interaction associated with the textbook culture. Another factor that could dilute these patterns is an improvement in the physical condition of schools. Most Indian schools continue to have poor quality buildings and very little teaching equipment. In elementary schools, the only teaching aid universally available is the prescribed textbook. According to the Fourth All India Educational Survey, 40 per cent of all primary schools have no blackboards, 53 per cent have no play space, 71 per cent have no libraries and 57 per cent are without concrete structures.[22]

The tension between local versus national concerns,

characteristic of the broad political context, has also been a key feature of curricular reforms since Independence. Reforms initiated by the government have mostly emphasised the generalised as opposed to the localised kinds of knowledge and symbols. This description would succinctly apply to the nature of curriculum reforms undertaken by the NCERT although its rhetoric seldom fails to suggest the contrary. During the fifties, curriculum policy was characterised by a conflict between the pull towards local relevance under Gandhian 'basic education' and the entrenched opposite pull towards centralisation. Gandhi's plan for educational reform was defeated both by ideological opposition to his vision of a self-reliant rural society and by deliberate attempts to make implementation ineffective. Textbook publishing houses were among the lobbies that made such attempts.

The trend towards centralised, as opposed to localised, development of curriculum and texts favours the continued use of prescribed textbooks as the dominant tool of pedagogy and as a symbol of the prescribing authority. This has led to a new contradiction. Schools are now expected to assist in the development of the child's total personality, and not just impart the basic skills as in the past. The new task demands the use of child-centred methods of teaching and decreased reliance on the prescribed textbooks. It also demands greater autonomy for teachers. This is the area where the new expectation from schools contradicts the pull towards further bureaucratisation and centralised management. Autonomy for teachers would imply greater professional self-reliance, demand for higher status, and local control. The fear of such demands continues to force the education system to reject the option of truly professionalising its teachers. Professionalising the school teacher would not just mean superior academic training; it would also mean conceding to the teacher the right to autonomy in matters pertaining to the choice of material for teaching and in the construction of the daily curriculum.

Notes

1. See Anil Seal, *The Emergence of Indian Nationalism* (Cambridge: Cambridge University Press, 1968), particularly the chapter on 'The Rewards of Education'. Also see R.E. Frykenberg, 'Education as an Instrument of Imperial Integration during the Company's Raj in South India', *Indo-British Review* 22 (June 1983): 58–85.
2. This was not very different from the way colonial rule worked in other societies. See P. Altbach and G. Kelly (eds.), *Education and Colonialism* (New York: Longmans, 1978).
3. For a comprehensive analysis of the status and role of education in a colonial, non-productive economy, see Asok Sen, *Iswar Chandra Vidyasagar and His Elusive Milestones* (Calcutta: Riddhi-India, 1977).
4. See the Second and Third Reports by William Adam, first published in 1836 and 1838 respectively. A new edition of these reports edited by Joseph di Bona is titled *One Teacher, One School* (New Delhi: Biblia Impex, 1983).
5. See, for instance, Rev. G. Milburn's article, 'Government and the Schools' in *The Indian Review* 15 (March 1914): 341–342. Also see Arthur Mayhew, *The Education of India* (London: Faber and Gwyer, 1926).
6. The amounts mentioned in this paragraph are given in the *Ninth Quinquennial Review* (*Vol. I*), *Progress of Education in India* 1992–27 (Calcutta: Government of India, Central Publication Branch, 1929).
7. See A.P. Howell's report, 'Education in British India, 1870–71' in *Selections from Educational Records of the Government of India, Vol. I* (Delhi: National Archives, 1960).
8. *The Statesman*, 1 January 1868. Fraser (full name, never mentioned, but in his writings, was J. Nelson Fraser).
9. For one account illustrating the influence, see 'Notes and Jottings' in *The Hindustan Review* 16 (October 1903): 364.
10. See J.A. Richey (ed), *Selections from Educational Records, Part II 1840–1859* (Delhi: National Archives, 1965): 301.

11. S. Shukla, 'Education, Economy and Social Structure in British India', *Varanasi National Journal of Education*, 1 (1 & 2: 1978): 112–125; 7–80.
12. J. Kerr, *Review of Public Instruction in the Bengal Presidency* (Calcutta: J. Thomas, 1852).
13. Kalyan K. Chatterjee, 'Mill and Macaulay on Indian Education', *Indo-British Review* 4 (4: 1972): 85–89.
14. Judith E. Welsh, *Growing Up in British India* (New York: Holmes & Meier, 1983).
15. Muriel Lester, *Gandhi, World Citizen* (Allahabad: Kitab Mahal 1962) 37.
16. For example, see the item 'A Novel Resolution' in *The Indian Review* 16 (Arpil 1915): 378, reporting the attempt made by E.R. Watson, a member of the Calcutta University Senate, to raise an alarm over the rise in the percentage of passes in the examination.
17. Two eminent examples are Premchand's 'Bare Bhai Saheb' (Big Brother), first published in 1933, and Chandra Bali Pathak's 'Pareeksha' (The Test), published in 1925 in *Balsakha*, a children's monthly.
18. Prakash Tandon, *Punjabi Century 1857–1947* (Berkeley: University of California Press, 1968).
19. L. Alston, *Education and Citizenship in India* (Bombay: Longmans, 1910) 63.
20. P.C. Ray, 'Scientific Instruction through the Vernaculars', *The Indian Review* (14 April 1913): 345–346.
21. Annie Besant, *India: Bond or Free?* (Madras: The Theosophical Publishing House, 1939).
22. *The Fourth All India Educational Survey* (New Delhi: NCERT, 1982).

3

Implications of a Divisive School System

In the first chapter we had briefly considered how the distribution of educational opportunities can affect the organisation of knowledge in the curriculum. In this chapter we will return to this point and examine it in terms of a somewhat different and deeper concern for school pedagogy. Briefly, the argument we will follow in this chapter is that the narrow spread of education and the divisive nature of the school system make the pursuit of humanist aims in pedagogy extremely difficult.

It is commonly believed that the quality of education in India has declined even as its 'quantity' or spread has increased. The late J.P. Naik had captured this in the title of his book, *Equality, Quality and Quantity: The Elusive Triangle in Indian Education*, published in the mid-seventies.[1] We are accustomed to seeing the tables of enrolment figures stacked up to defend the system of education against even a hint of a charge of a fall in standards. The tables do not, of course, defend the system directly, but they do provide a kind of emotional back-up. They are meant to suggest that we have been busy taking education to the masses. But, this may have left us no time to worry about maintaining high standards. The argument that flows from this understanding is that today our education has very little capacity to produce excellence because the system has spread so widely.

But, the argument pursued here is the opposite, namely that our education system has remained backward because it is so narrow. I call it 'backward' for a widely accepted reason, which is its low capacity to produce or encourage excellence. This is true not just for science, technology, and the social sciences, where the inputs needed for the pursuit of excellence are somewhat complex, but also for sports where the necessary inputs are of a fairly straightforward variety. Even here, countries with fewer people to choose from and with lower levels of development routinely beat us. If one of the functions of education is to harness excellence, then surely our education system can appropriately be called backward. The roots of our education system's backwardness lie in its narrowness.

Although the facilities for education have enormously expanded since Independence, the system continues to be 'narrow' in three distinct senses. The more obvious sense pertains to its coverage. Literacy figures are an indicator of the system's reach, but the more telling figures are those indicating the rate of drop-outs at the primary level. Out of every 100 students who enrol in grade one, only 37 attend grade five. All those proceeding beyond this stage must learn and socialise in a reduced human environment. The maximum fall occurs between grade one and two—a point to which we will return for some detailed probing in the next chapter. Out of every 100 children who enrol in grade one, 37 stop coming to school some time during the first year or, at any rate, do not show up for grade two. This phenomenon, generally known as the 'drop-out rate', has remained largely unaffected by all the progress claimed in the area of elementary education over the last two decades. The primary school has continued to function as an agency of relentless elimination. It makes sure that the literate Indian will remain part of a minority, and the educated Indian will remain part of an even narrower minority.

The second aspect of the narrowness of our education system has to do with a division within the limited number of children who manage to go to school and continue there. The division consists of two sub-systems—the 'common' and the 'exclusive'. The first sub-system consists of children who depend on the state for their school education, and the second of those whose education is paid for by their parents. The coexistence of these two parallel schools ensures that children of the better-off are separated early from the children of the poor. The separation occurs as a part of the rites of admission to the second category of schools. These schools represent the 'open market' where urban, white-collar parents can buy 'good quality' education for their children. The schools of the first category, on the contrary, represent the state sector. As a welfare agency, the state gives little assurance to the white-collar class, even to its bottom rungs, that the expectations of this class will not drown amidst the far more pressing demands of the vast majority consisting of the labouring masses. Moreover, the white-collar, middle-class parent is anxious to 'protect' his child from the rougher world of the children of the poor. This anxiety is the source of the drive and finances to start private schools in every nook and corner of urban India.

This anxiety of the educated middle class is, of course, not something new; only, it is now finding a sharper expression than earlier. Let us briefly place this anxiety in a historical context. The dynamics of colonial rule meant that the lower strata of society would aspire for the same educational and employment opportunities as the upper strata had. In many parts of British India, the struggle against colonial rule took the form of an urge for upward mobility among the lower strata of the population.[2] Organised expression of this aspiration in several parts of British

India, particularly in its major towns, presented a serious problem to the propertied and professional classes. Many members of these classes, and certainly the leaders, had been inspired by the equality-oriented ideology of English utilitarians. At the same time, they had to protect their dominant position in the established social structure.

The ideology of utilitarianism itself provided the answer to this conflict. The utilitarian model of democracy had projected the market as the locus of egalitarian values. In the context of education, this meant the individual's right to invest in the maintenance of private schools. In any case, the colonial government rarely lost an opportunity to praise any initiatives on the part of the native community to set up schools. The Victorian ideal of 'self-help' gave moral verve to governmental approval, and the art of imperial budgeting for the colony provided the financial rationale. The combination of the government's appeal on the one hand, and the anxiety of the propertied classes on the other, led to the emergence of separate institutions for the children of these classes. The model for such institutions came from England's famous residential public schools. The early attempts to establish such schools in India were made by English administrators and Indian feudal interests in the latter half of the nineteenth century. By the early decades of the twentieth century, the aim of setting up public schools in India had crystallised enough to bring together feudal and commercial interest groups. The list of contributors to the Indian Public Schools Society for the opening of the Doon School included both the groups.

The exclusive character of Indian public schools was clear enough, but the utilitarian veneer of a belief in equality was never dropped. What helped to maintain it was the idea of meritocracy. Scholarships were provided for children who were found eligible in 'merit' tests but whose parents could not afford the tuition and other fees of a public school. The concept of 'merit' included both curriculum-related abilities and behaviour that reflected an upbringing in a propertied or middle-class environment. These are the criteria that all types of present-day exclusive schools use to legitimate their right to select children. The political climate of contemporary India forbids any institution to show the slightest sign of bias towards the higher strata of society. The pressure to appear democratic hangs heavy. A policy of enrolment by competition suits this air, and also solves the problem of the propertied and the urban middle classes. It permits the parents of these classes to give the necessary inputs to their children in their early childhood years to meet the requirements of 'merit'-detecting school tests for enrolment. The idea of a competitive entry is indeed so functional in the late twentieth century Indian ethos, that the central government has jumped into the fray to provide privileged residential schooling to the 'meritorious'. This is what gives the Navodaya scheme its populist political character.

A key feature of all types of exclusive or elite schools is that their students live in a restricted universe. The elite school selects its clientele out of the larger population, and thereby constructs a narrow sphere within which its clientele must socialise. This practice alienates the school from its milieu. Wherever admission policy departs from the principle of neighbourhood, school population ceases to represent the social reality around. This would be true anywhere in the world, but it is more sharply true in a society like ours where every milieu is economically heterogeneous. The wealthy Indian likes exclusiveness, and so does the middle class, but neither can manage without domestic servants and a whole range of other services. Since each mansion has a servant's quarter and a nearby slum, the out-of-school environment of an Indian child invariably consists of both riches and poverty. This applies just as well to villages as it does to cities. This is why when a school closes its door to the poor, it ceases to be a part of the milieu.

This constitutes a major pedagogical drawback for our elite schools. They cannot use their milieu as a learning resource simply because the milieu contradicts their attempt to construct a homogeneous universe within their barbed wire boundaries. Use of a foreign language as the medium of instruction is only a symbolic manifestation of the elite school's overall attempt to alienate itself from the milieu. The functional alienation, implying the impossibility of drawing upon the school's milieu, is far more acute

Before discussing how this alienation affects pedagogy and the pursuit of quality, let me move to a third, philosophical sense in which our education system is narrow. This third indicator of narrowness has to do with the concept of the human being underlying education. Educators remind young people every day that education must refer to the whole human being—or to the human personality in the widest sense of the term. Let us consider for a moment what this worship is all about. At one level it refers to the qualities we associate with human nature, qualities which have enabled mankind to achieve all that it has achieved in its long history. At another level, it refers to the basic unity of all mankind, and this unity is nothing if it does not include equality of all men and women on certain basic criteria related to the conditions that are necessary for human survival. So, in education when we refer to the whole human being we mean those aspects which apply to all. We want the child to know his humanity, realise his potential as a human being, also, we want him to respect the humanity that lies in every person, and to know how to treat others as fellow human beings, irrespective of their personal weaknesses, colour of skin, and sex, let alone their social status and income.

We can hardly dream of moving towards this aim in a school whose admission policy consciously aims at homogeneity of social class, ability, or behaviour. It may offer a high quality of rigorous instruction, but its instruction will not answer the child's search for meaning. This is because meaning arises in interaction with other human beings. One's relatedness to other people is what creates the context in which acts of inquiry become meaningful. Such a context remains permanently stunted or underdeveloped in a school which has a restrictive admission policy. This kind of school negates the very idea of the relatedness of human beings. A school that has only one segment of the wider society represented in it is greatly depleted in terms of a human context. Its children are forced to seek the relevance of their activities in a narrow sphere of interactions. What is relevant except the truth of inquiry in relation to life?

Lacking a rich human environment, the elite school seeks to inspire its children with unending opportunities for competition and achievement. Institutional loyalty and personal achievement are presented as interlinked motives. Children are encouraged to compete individually from day one at school on the grounds that their competitive spirit will bring glory to the school. Thus, personal aggrandisement is legitimised in the name of institutional goals in the same way that the market economy validates possessive individualism by referring to the national good. Elite schools serve the market economy by socialising children to believe in the goodness of possessive individualism. Serving this role, however, makes them vulnerable to a serious contradiction.

The contradiction lies in the elite school's emphasis on competition and meritocracy on the one hand, and its hankering after modern, progressive methods of pedagogy on the other. Progressive ideas in pedagogy, since Froebel, demand that children be treated as children—as autonomous, free people, rather than as raw material to be moulded after stale preconceptions that adults might have. In the latter half of the twentieth century, progressive pedagogies have come to stand more firmly on this view of the child than ever before because now they have scientifically developed knowledge of the child to back them. After Piaget, all rationalist and instrumentalist notions of curriculum and teaching have no steam left in them. Piaget's work has made it possible for an adult to think on behalf of the child, and to appreciate what learning means to the child. The implication of Piagetian theories is clear—that learning takes its own time; that it may be destructive to speed up learning or development.[3]

Such an idea is totally against the pedagogy and ethic of the competitive elite school. With its commitment to egging the child on to higher and still higher levels of achievement and competition with others, the elite school naturally treats time in an instrumentalist manner, i.e., as a commodity. According to this perception, time can be compressed, and children can be made to learn more and faster than they might do on their own. With this philosophy, elite schools cannot offer what David Elkind, famous American child psychologist, says is absolutely crucial to sound learning—'large blocks of time in which the child can totally engross himself in an activity.' Pressure to learn faster and to outshine others kills all intrinsic motivation to learn. What remains is that urge to make the teacher and parents feel happy and proud of you. Intellectually, most children studying in our prestigious city schools are burned out by the end of the primary grades.

It is hardly surprising that despite their privileged status, their access to the best of materials and equipment, and their freedom to deal only with the allegedly brighter children, our elite schools have not produced world-class talent. They have produced any number of bureaucrats, military officers, managers, businessmen and journalists, but how prideworthy is their contribution to science and technology, sports, and the arts? One or two names like Homi Bhabha aside, the record is poor. For understandable reasons, the merit lists of elite schools lack the names of great litterateurs in Indian languages, but why do they lack names of people who might be expected to make breakthroughs in science and technology, architecture and the arts? Why haven't the elite schools mitigated our backwardness as a nation, our dependence in every sphere on the advanced countries for ideas and inspiration?

To a certain extent, the answer to this question lies in the overall curriculum and culture of our elite schools. Following the example of British public schools, our own public schools, and later on other elite schools, emphasised institutional loyalty, liberal interests and sports, at the expense of individual excellence in specialised academic fields. They also discouraged the pursuit of knowledge for the sake of any practical use. As Wiener points out in the case of British public schools, our elite schools too produced any number of administrators and military men, but very few eminent scientists, engineers and industrial entrepreneurs.[4] Strange though it sounds, there is reason to see our public school culture as the agency through which the attitudes and values of England's landed aristocracy have cast a lasting spell on our elite. The recent emergence of a powerful competitive ethic has not influenced this legacy. The function of this ethic was to maintain exclusiveness and high status, not to encourage specialised excellence. In any case, the *competitive* ethic could not possibly have provided the impetus for individual excellence as I have explained above.

On the strength of its recognition and status in society, the elite school sets the ethos and pace for pedagogical practices in the common schools. Indeed, the common schools have no choice except to imitate the elite schools as best as they can. Already depleted in terms of resources and material, the common schools make life more oppressive for the child by copying the competitive ethic of elite schools, along with the obsession for individual achievement and the fetish of institutional prestige at ceremonial events. Yet another factor that diminishes the common school's ability to provide children with genuine opportunities for learning is the demoralisation of its teachers. In fact, both teachers and children in ordinary schools now feel that however hard they may try, they cannot expect anything better than second-rate success. This feeling is likely to become more strong in the years to come as the elite sector expands even within the government system, offering special privilege and status to its clientele.

By nurturing the elite sector and by allowing it to influence the common schools, we have closed all options for progressive pedagogy to flourish in our midst. The elite school has proved incapable of freeing itself from its colonial archetype, and the common school has become demoralised. There is hardly any room left for progressive pedagogies within either system. Outside education, the socio-political and economic climate favour the continuation of dependency and neo-colonial relationships. The economic level is the central arena in which dependency and underdevelopment are expressed, but their roots lie in the educational and cultural climate. As I have argued above, oppression of the child, and rejection of his right to autonomy are the main features of the educational climate which contribute to the backwardness of our cultural and economic life. We rewrite the contract of our dependence every morning in our oppressive schools.

I will end this discussion by looking at how the separation of the rich children from the poor, and that of the supposedly bright from the average, makes certain key reforms in education impossible. My explanation hinges on the distinction between sponsored and context mobilities.[5] Although the Indian political system supports context mobility and emphasises equal educational opportunity, the continuation of elite schools keeps the avenues of sponsored mobility open. It is well known how the different types of elite school systems offer to their clientele routes of sponsored mobility to elite jobs. The routes pass through elite institutions at the higher education level. From nursery onwards, there is a network of exclusive institutions which allows the elite to maintain their position of advantage.

Such a network would have met with serious threats from mass-based politics if there had been no mechanism in the education system to counterbalance it. The mechanism which serves precisely this function is the system of examinations. While exclusive schools and colleges ensure special treatment to the children of the wealthy, mass examinations promise total parity among all candidates. Examinations carry the message of equality in exactly those features such as secrecy of the identity of the paper-setter and evaluators, strict invigilation at the time when examinees write answers, impersonal marking and delayed declaration of results. While exclusive institutions make sure that the elite have the means to provide privileged treatment to their children, mass examinations—featuring strict parity among examinees—keep the confidence and aspirations of the masses alive. Thus status-based streaming and mass examinations are two conflicting characteristics that together endorse the legitimacy of our education system.[6]

Historically, mass examinations served the function of evolving a bureaucratic system of education. They implied uniformity of standards and expectations. In the early period of the development of our education system, examinations provided to the rising middle class a sense of hope and belief in the fairness of the colonial order. While elite schools provided safe routes towards status professions to the children of the privileged families, mass examinations offered to the rest of the society the assurance that status can also be achieved through competition. The examination system could offer this assurance with credibility because it was so ritualised. It required students to rehearse endlessly the familiar skills that was necessary to enter the newly introduced channels of secure jobs in the service of the colonial government. As the civil service was the major elite goal to which education was expected to lead, all examinations became preparatory and therefore similar, in terms of requirements, to the competitive examinations for civil service jobs. This association kept the curriculum stable which was confined to the prescribed syllabus and textbooks.

The basic character of our examination system has not changed to this day. Examinations continue to focus on the capacities to memorise and reproduce, and consequently, classroom instruction too concentrates on these capacities. Indeed, the examination system keeps both curriculum and classroom teaching in its grip. Even the most imaginative teachers, few as they are, find it hard not to succumb sooner or later to the demand that they should teach for the examinations. The demand never dies even among students, although they may have experienced the joy of learning under a spirited teacher. It is unlikely that the examination system can be changed as long as the structure within which examinations serve a social function remains intact. If early selection (on whatever grounds) and sponsored mobility continue to be openly and widely practised, examinations too will continue to be what they are, i.e., a means of testing the ability to copy from memory. And they will overcome any attempts that might be made by well-intentioned planners to reform curriculum and instruction towards greater dynamism and innovativeness. If we hate to have such sterile curricula, such lifeless methodologies of teaching, we ought to know that the supportive cause of such pedagogical backwardness is in the divided structure of our education system.

Notes

1. J.P. Naik, *Equality, Quality and Quantity: The Elusive Triangle in Indian Education* (New Delhi: Allied, 1975).
2. For instance, English education policies were greeted with enormous enthusiasm by the oppressed castes of Maharashtra. See Dhananjay Keer's *Mahatma Jyoti ba Phooley, Father of Our Social Revolution* (Bombay: Popular, 1964).
3. An analysis of the implications of speeding up learning and emotional growth can be found in *The Hurried Child* (Reading, Mass: Addison-Wesley, 1981) by David Elkind.
4. Martin J. Wiener, *English Culture and the Decline of the Industrial Spirit, 1950–1980*, (Cambridge: Cambridge University Press, 1981).
5. See R.H. Turner, 'Sponsored and Context Mobility and the School System', *American Sociological Review*, 25 (6 : December 1960): 855–67.
6. For a more detailed discussion of this dialectic, see my 'Reproduction or Change? Education and Elites in India', in *Education and the Process of Change* (New Delhi: Sage, 1987), edited by R. Ghosh and M. Zachariah.

4

Reading in the Primary School Curriculum

How many more illiterates will India have, and what percentage of the world's illiterates are from India since the beginning of this millennium? Answers to these dramatic questions form the staple statistical themes of conference speeches. Evidently, our performance in the pursuit of mass literacy is the central concern of our dismal system of education. The expansion of the education system has not had any striking impact on literacy. While primary education has expanded as given data show—3.3 times during the four decades following Independence—the percentage of literates in the total population has just about doubled itself, and that too with dilution in the norms of recording literacy-related skills in census surveys. Why has primary education performed so poorly?

The search for explanations has typically been made in the context of the economic conditions prevailing in rural India. The question why primary schools fail to retain children long enough to make them permanently literate is usually explained away by referring to the poverty of rural parents. Studies leaning on the 'culture of poverty' concept continue to hold sway, and they tell us that poor parents 'withdraw' their children from school mainly because they are too poor to afford to have children at school rather than at work. Rarely does anyone wonder if primary school pedagogy could have something to do with the school's failure to retain children long enough to make them literate. This is the direction I will pursue here in search of an explanation for the poor performance of primary education in the context of literacy. I will argue that the entrenched pedagogy of reading may be at the heart of the problem of early elimination from school.

Early Elimination

India's education system does not cover all children of the primary school age (i.e., 6 to 11 years). Precisely what proportion of children it covers is a matter of some controversy. School enrolment figures for grades one to five, compiled by the Department of Education, convey the impression that nearly 90 per cent of the 6–11 year olds in the country are enrolled in primary schools or non-formal institutions. The recently released selected statistics of the Fifth All India Educational Survey further strengthen this impression. Prominent among the researchers who questioned the impression is Yash Aggarwal,[1] who pursued the same field that John Kurrien[2] had worked on earlier, and which showed the large difference between the figures of enrolment given by the Department of Education and those collected by the census. Going by the responses collected under the 1981 census, Aggarwal concludes that only 47 per cent of the children of primary school age are actually in schools, either formal or non-formal. Out of the rest, perhaps quite a few are enrolled but they are not attending school. The discrepancy between census data and enrolment data is very wide indeed. The government's pressure on teachers to enrol every child in the community can be accounted for by referring to the high rate of elimination (official term 'dropping out') from school. Indeed, the two explanations complement each other. Teachers enrol children under orders from above, but fail to keep them at school. This is what the well-studied phenomenon of 'dropping out' is all about. Earlier planners, most prominently the late J.P. Naik, used to call it the wastage rate, for they thought that the resources spent on a child who leaves school before completing a stage are wasted. Naik had worked out the wastage rate to be about 60 per cent between grades one and five, i.e., out of 100 children enrolled in grade one only 40 reach grade five.[3]

There is no reason to think that this rate has declined. Apparently, collection of age- and grade-wise enrolment data was discontinued in the early seventies.[4] This may be why the statistical appendix to the document called 'Challenge of Education', which outlined the perspective for the 1986 education policy, was content to carry a table (compiled in 1983) showing grade-wise enrolment rates up to the 1970–78 batch of elementary school-going population.[5] According to this table, the national average of elimination between grades one and five was 66 per cent. In other words, out of the 100 children who enrolled in 1970–71 in grade one, only 34 remained until grade five. Of the 66 who left, 39 had already done so within the first year, resulting in 61 per cent enrolment in grade two (compared to grade one). These rates of elimination seem to have remained quite stable, which implies that the general processes of socio-economic development and change have not had much impact in this matter.

Widespread and stable though the phenomenon of early elimination has been, it continues to be rather poorly understood. The general belief is that economic pressures on children and parents of 'backward' socio-economic strata are responsible for the high incidence of premature school leaving. This belief gains support from the fact that child labour is very common in India. Children's usefulness as cheap and readily available labour is widely cited in social and demographic research to explain why school enrolment does not remain stable during the elementary years. No less than 500 studies have been listed in a recent annotated bibliography on the so-called 'drop-out' rate.[6] With few exceptions, these studies conclude that poverty drives parents to withdraw their children from school. The assumptions underlying the majority of these studies are clear enough. The major assumption is that early elimination is caused by poverty and backwardness. The argument is simple: since almost all children who leave school early are poor, this kind of behaviour ought to be related to poverty.

No study has yet explained why the child's labour value changes dramatically between grade one and two where the elimination rate is highest. As the enrolment data given earlier indicate, 39 out of the 66 children (per 100) who stop attending school between grades one and five do so within grade one. In other words, nearly 61 per cent of the 'drop-out' children belong to the youngest age group attending school. Most likely, these children are five to seven years old. Now, if these children are leaving school because of the economic necessity of their families, there ought to be a sudden increase in the children's capacity for work between grades one and two, roughly age six to seven. Surely we need a medical explanation for this sudden jump. Otherwise, why would a parent send this child to grade one but withdraw him before grade two? The question takes the bottom out of the theory that early elimination has a satisfactory economic explanation in our conditions in the late twentieth century. It also questions the research convention of asking poor parents why they withdraw their children from school. The basis of such interviewing lies in the 'culture of poverty' theory which continues to influence social research in India.

It is time we turned our attention to the child's perspective on this problem. One of the questions we should ask if we took the child's perspective is: 'Does the primary school provide what a grade one child is looking for?' The paramount motivation in a grade one child is to make sense of the world around him. Poor health, malnutrition, and oppressive control of the child's routine can weaken this drive but they cannot wipe it out. The child of six, irrespective of his existential conditions, is curious about the world, and wants to manipulate and understand it One of the primary means of doing these things is language, and a grade one child is already familiar with its marvellous capacities. He has already used it to establish relationships, to internalise these relationships, and then to apply the internalisation to explore a wider world.[7] Along with movement, touch, vision, hearing, and smell, a child of six is familiar with the exciting possibilities of language. He knows from social lore that school is where he will learn two new powerful skills namely, reading and writing, and much else.

We can hardly capture the associations of growth, power, and knowledge that the five-plus child makes with the school before entering it. If we are able to hold even a small fraction of these associations in our view, we would know how frustrated the child must get after he has spent a few days at an average primary school. He would find out that the school is not the place where he can 'make sense' of the world. Skills that any child would use to solve new problems have no place in the grade one class. Indeed, 'making sense' and 'solving problems' are not on the agenda at all. What is on the agenda, to begin with, is to learn the shapes of letters that form the syllabary, and to know the names by which they are called. The child is required to master the syllabary by sounding out the names of all the letters and practise writing them correctly over and over again. When the syllabary has been mastered in this manner, the child is called upon to recognise the different letters forming a word given in the primer, and to pronounce the word. The words he is asked to confront at this stage are part of a long convention of pedagogy, and have nothing to do with a child's perception or curiosity.

Moreover, the school has hardly anything that the child is free to touch, manipulate, and examine. The Fourth All India Educational Survey showed that over 50 per cent of primary schools in India did not have a concrete structure, playground, or even a drinking-water facility, 40 per cent were without blackboards, and 70 per cent had no library of any kind. The school is a colourless, alienated, stuffy little place from the point of view of a six year old. Any excuse would be good enough to stop going there.

Literacy and Meaning

This reconstruction leads us to hypothesise that the pedagogy of language, particularly reading, may be at the heart of the problem of early elimination. The manner in which our primary schools attempt to impart the capacity to read could well hold an explanation that we have not heard yet. This explanation does not negate the validity of other explanations, such as the ones related to poverty and child labour. There can be no doubt about the impact of destitution and hunger in the family on school attendance. The point is to prepare a model consisting of all the salient features of the phenomenon. The few researchers who have paid some attention to the pedagogical conditions of primary schools have treated them as a peripheral aspect of the overall picture. It may be worthwhile to look at pedagogy more carefully, particularly the pedagogy of reading and writing. These are the two foundation skills on which the edifice of the school's system of teaching and certifying rests. Also, competence in reading and writing determines the child's ability to benefit from the information storage systems that are characteristic of a literate society. The school system as we know it today is a key agency serving literacy-based information storage systems essential for modern social organisation. If the school fails to impart literacy with lasting effect to a great proportion of its students, it must be seen as a case of serious institutional dysfunction in the overall social system. We have reason to believe that such a dysfunction has occurred in our country. Early elimination rates are one indication of this. It is self-evident that the majority of children who enrol for primary education abandon it without acquiring lasting literacy. Of the children who continue to study, a great many do not acquire the ability to comprehend what they read. The dismal performance of Indian students in the IEA tests only proves what every secondary school and college teacher knows from daily experience.[8]

In the sphere of reading, the common practices applied in our primary schools sharply contrast with what scientific knowledge about the reading process suggests. The general state of the teaching of reading in grade one is close to what contemporary reading researchers would identify as the 'traditional' approach. In brief, this approach is characterised by the treatment of script as a complex package of information to be learnt for its own sake. Children must learn the names of different letters, and they must develop the ability to recognise them separately and as part of a word. Only after this familiarity with letters becomes reliable is the child allowed to apply it on a sentence representing a meaningful statement. This takes time, for the process involves a considerable amount of mechanical work which offers no immediate pay-off or satisfaction. Reading is treated in this approach as an end product, which the child must wait for, suspending his desire to find meaning in written material, especially to find meaning with which he can relate.

Current research on the reading process tells us that the desire to relate and to find meaning are at the heart of reading.[9] It is now understood that reading and writing skills represent later stages of the continuum on which symbolic interaction through talk, play, and drawing appear earlier. The continuum encapsulates the child's desire to be involved in communication. We cannot isolate the tasks involved in reading from this continuum without seriously altering the nature of these tasks. If we teach children to recognise letters as an isolated task, we influence the nature and the role of this task in the overall process of reading. Children breaking down words into letters, and sentences into words are a common sight in Indian primary schools. Those who do so internally may far outnumber the ones who do so verbally, and this category could well be applied to many adult members of the literate population. For a child who has learnt to read letter by letter or word by word, there is no choice except to recode the text into a sound system which then has to be decoded via the phonological, syntactic, and semantic components.[10] It is an arduous and necessarily wasteful process which overloads the child's short-term memory and the capacity to pay attention to meaning.

There is of course a chance that children taught to read by the traditional methods may also become competent readers. The presence of a loving and encouraging teacher can imbue any process, however mechanical, with a sense of worth. This would be especially true if the teacher has all the time in the world to work with the child. One suspects that this condition was at work during the years when only a few people were required to possess literacy skills. Availability of leisure, freedom from competition, and the small number of pupils for a teacher were the other complementary conditions that made the traditional approaches of imparting reading skills reasonably successful. These conditions were characteristic of a society whose culture sanctioned an elite to monopolise the means of using literacy and the means to store accumulated knowledge, particularly knowledge about the society's past. In such a society, a teacher could well afford to expand the process of learning to be literate in every possible mechanical detail. In turning the phonology and the graphology of the language into a full-blown curriculum, he did not have to worry about imparting a sense of meaning at every stage. In the cultural milieu we are referring to, a sense of meaning need not have been a part of the daily learning experience, for meaning was generated elsewhere, for example in the association between educational opportunity and high social status.

We confront an altogether different set of circumstances today, under which the persistence of traditional methods of reading and writing present a case of cultural anachronism. Industrial development and the socio-political institutions that are conducive to industrialisation demand mass education, especially mass literacy. Industrialisation breaks down the collective meanings and sources of self-respect that an oral culture might offer to its members. Particularly under capitalism, industrial development forces all members of society to generate meanings by individual effort, and to be prepared to surrender self-respect if the meanings thus generated do not help one stay afloat in the market economy. Some societies have succeeded to a certain extent in softening this power of industrial development by projecting national identity and ideology as reservoirs to which individuals can turn for deriving a sense of worth. But even these societies have not neglected the task of assisting the individual child to generate a sense of personal meaning through education. This is the reason why child-centred methods of education have been accepted as essential not just in the bourgeois United States but also in the former socialist Soviet Union. The significance of these methods lies in the capacities they have for sustaining mass motivation for learning and for making sense of situations. The methods were born out of the needs created by industrialisation, and they continue to serve industrial development, both by imparting universal and effective literacy, and by sustaining the individual's desire to live and make sense of conditions brought about by the advancement of industrialisation.

Cheaper Sector?

The problem in a country like ours is that it wants to industrialise without investing in primary schools. So we continue to keep the primary school in conditions that make child-centred methods inapplicable. The naming of the recent, much-publicised 'Operation Blackboard' shows how badly the state has treated primary education all along.[11] The fact is that in India, as in many other so-called developing countries, primary education has been customarily regarded as a cheaper sector in comparison to secondary and higher education. This view of primary education is reflected in the inter-sectoral gap that exists in educational financing of the richer, developed and developing countries of the world. Whereas in higher education, the richer countries make five times greater per capita investment than what the poorer countries make, in primary education the richer countries spend thirty times more than what the poorer countries do per child.[12]

Another manifestation of the view that primary education can do with lower-order resources can be found in the educational budget since the fifties. As compared with 1950–51 when primary education accounted for 40 per cent of the expenditure incurred on education as a whole, in 1979–80 it accounted for only 24 per cent. Plan allocation for primary education similarly declined from 56 per cent in the First Plan to 29 per cent in the Seventh Plan.[13] This decline becomes particularly meaningful if we place it against the continual increase of India's child population and the increase in the number of primary schools. Compared to the 150,000 primary schools that India had at the time of Independence, there were about 500,000 at the beginning of the 1990s. The implication is clear—that educational policy did emphasise expansion of primary education but permitted the thinning of resources allocated for it.

During the 1990s, Indian primary education received unprecedented financial backing in the context of the structural adjustment of the economy to the world capitalist system. International aid and soft loans became available for both expansion and the improvement of quality under the auspices of the District Primary Education Programme.[14] For a little while it looked as if the entrenched perception of primary education as a responsibility to be met with the lowest possible investment will give way to a more realistic idea of the funds required. This expectation proved illusory, and before anyone knew what was happening, cheaper options began to take root in areas like teachers' salaries, which were earlier regarded as non-negotiable. State after state took the option of appointing para-teachers who would cost the state far less than regular teachers. Money was saved not only on salaries but on training requirements as well, as the scheme of para-teachers envisaged an extremely brief, necessarily token training. Instead of offering an opportunity for a breakthrough, international financial support for primary education opened the floodgates of corruption in the selection of para-teachers at the village and district levels, and in a variety of other procedures. When the external support dries up—it was meant for a seven-year cycle—it is anybody's guess how the system will cope with the continued paucity of national commitment to primary education and the funds it demands. The latest initiative called the Sarva Shiksha Abhiyan offers no relief from the older, confused and manipulative policies which deny the children of India, especially the poorest, any substantial right to primary education though a constitutional amendment has granted such a right on paper.

If primary education is to be regarded in future as a key agency for achieving mass literacy, then the perception of primary education as a cheaper sector will have to change. Early schooling of a kind that offers children an absorbing environment and a real chance to become literate implies an expensive model. Such a model will mean extensive equipping of primary classrooms with material objects. The creation of appropriate spaces for learning and play equipment will be the first requirement, followed by an ongoing supply of equipment. At the moment, manufacturing of primary-level learning resources is part of a rather poorly developed small-scale industry. Certain sectors of the industry, such as the manufacturing of indigenous toys, are under great stress. In other sectors, such as the manufacturing of modern play devices, and children's books, there is both a lack of direction and absence of norms. Regeneration of primary education cannot materialise without the investment of very substantial monetary and organisational resources in the manufacturing of pedagogical materials. What gives this condition an added significance is the prevalence of the 'textbook culture' which we have discussed earlier. A product of colonisation, this culture encourages school pedagogy to stay literally within the specific lessons of the prescribed textbook. Poverty of the primary school exacerbates the rigidity and thinness of classroom work. The dominance of prescribed textbooks can be expected to abate if the manufacture and supply of pedagogical resources, especially of children's literature, improves.

The equipping of primary schools for curricular enrichment also requires modernisation of teacher training and change in the career conditions of primary-level teachers. At present, the primary teacher is a powerless and poorly paid professional functionary of the education system. One implication of the primary teacher's powerless position in the system is the absence of opportunities for the exercise of judgement and imagination in matters like curriculum and preparation of text materials. This situation is exacerbated by the bleak pre-service training available for primary teachers. What academic content it has is largely obsolete, and its skill-related component lacks practical value for actual classroom settings. Literacy teaching is a particularly weak area of teacher-training curricula. Recent research and theorisations in the areas of reading and writing are largely unknown in Indian teacher training institutions, although at some of them, one can find a part of the staff parroting the recent Western jargon. What puts the icing on this sad situation is the old belief that teachers need only skills, not theory. This belief makes the recent advances in reading research irrelevant for us, for the major implication of this research is that the teachers must understand the theory underlying recommended practices. A teacher who is ignorant of the theory behind ideas, such as building a classroom ethos conducive to individual interpretation and intelligent guessing, is unlikely to be able to build such an ethos.

Changes in classroom conditions along the lines indicated here are incompatible with the powerlessness of the teacher and the poverty of resources available for primary schools. How will these features of the present system permit an alternative model to gain acceptance? The question forces us to remember that perceptions of education are rooted in the political economy of a society and therefore cannot be radically altered in isolation. A certain degree of change in the state's level of concern for primary education is all that we can hope for, if sufficient pressure on the state is built up. In the pursuit of this restricted aim, we may do well by reminding those who hold state power that steps to improve primary education may not necessarily involve social conflict. Acharya has indicated the possibility of discontent arising among the richer farmers if effective primary schooling obstructs the supply of cheap child labour.[15] It is unlikely that the discontent of the richer farmers will find expression in violence or further oppression, but even if it does in some cases, the 'risk' does not justify the state's unpreparedness for investing larger resources in primary education, unless the state is merely an instrument of the richer strata of society.

Notes

1. Yash Aggarwal, 'Towards Education for all Children: Intent and Reality', *Journal of Educational Planning and Administration*, 2 (1 & 2: 1988): 69–106.
2. John Kurrien, *Elementary Education in India: Myth, Reality, Alternatives* (New Delhi: Vikas, 1983).
3. J.P. Naik, *Elementary Education in India, A Promise to Keep* (New Delhi: Allied, 1975).
4. See 'Editorial' of *Journal of Educational Planning and Administration* in the issue referred to under note 1.
5. This appendix was apparently withdrawn soon after publication. A Hindi translation of this appendix is available in *Palash* (a journal supported by the Madhya Pradesh Government) in its October-November 1985 issue.
6. Problems of School Drop-outs in India, an Annotated Bibliography prepared by B.R. Patil, (New Delhi: Council for Social Development, 1984).
7. See L.S. Vygotsky, *Thought and Language* (Cambridge, Mass: MIT, 1962) and Joan Tough, *The Development of Meaning* (London: Routledge, Kegan & Paul, 1977).
8. R.L. Thorndike, *Reading Comprehension Education in Fifteen Countries* (Stockholm: Alonquist & Wiksell, 1972).
9. For an overview of recent reading research, see Cliff Moon, 'Recent Developments in the Teaching of Reading' in *English in Education* (18 1: 1984): 20–27. Also see D.R. Olson, N. Torrance and A. Hildyard (eds.) *Literacy, Language, and Learning* (Cambridge: Cambridge University Press, 1984) and R. Glaser, 'Cognitive

Science and Education' *International Journal of Social Science* 255 (115: 1988): 21–44.

10. G.C. Elias and D.E. Ingram, *Cultural Components of Reading* (Singapore: Singapore University Press, 1977).
11. See my 'Breaking Away' in *Future* (11–12, 1984): 34–39, for an overview of the condition of primary schools.
12. *Education Sector Policy Paper* (World Bank, 1980).
13. See J.B.G. Tilak, *Political Economy of Education in India* (Mimeo. 1989).
14. For a critical analysis of this programme, see Krishna Kumar, Manisha Priyam, Sadhna Saxena, 'Looking Beyond the Smokescreen', *Economic and Political Weekly* (36: 7, 17 February 2001): 560–68.
15. Poromesh Acharya, 'Roots of Bengal's Illiteracy', *Future* (11–12, 1984) 56–59.

5

Storytelling: What is the Use?

It is a great pity that our primary schools do not have a separate 'period' for storytelling for the first two grades each day. Such a provision would have solved at least a part of the problem we face in retaining children at school. Many will say that I am giving undue importance to this problem. I can well imagine many senior officers smiling cynically at my suggestion. Their vast experience and administrative wisdom have erased from their minds the knowledge I am sure they once possessed, that storytelling has a magical effect on children. It is terribly sad that even our teacher-training institutes do not take storytelling seriously although some of them do remember to mention its importance during the course of training. I should like to imagine the day when anyone who wants to teach young children will be required to master at least thirty traditional stories. By 'master' I mean: to know the stories by heart, so one can tell them in a relaxed, confident manner. That is hardly a tall order for a society that has inherited thousands of stories from its past. Thirty stories that the teacher can tell at will can transform the ethos of the first two years of primary schooling, provided of course that the daily curriculum finds an honourable place for storytelling for its own sake.

In the preceding paragraph I have used an adjective which I

must explain before proceeding further. I have said that I favour traditional stories. My experience of training young teachers in the art of storytelling is that when they are asked to look for stories to tell, they usually come up with stories published in a magazine for children or stories depicted as comics, and sometimes even longish jokes and narratives of real events. Now, of course, all such material comes under the broad category called 'story' but not all such material can be expected to do the kind of magic we are hoping to perform with six or seven year olds in a primary school. Stories that have come down to us from tradition have a special set of characteristics that contemporary stories presented in different forms and in the media do not necessarily possess. We shall soon see what these characteristics are, but let me first name a few sources of traditional stories. The *Panchatantra*, the *Jatakas*, the *Mahabharat*, the *Arabian Nights*, stories of Vikramditya, and folktales from different regions come to mind as ready and rich sources. Then there are other selections like the *Kathasaritsagar*, the *Gulistan* and the *Bostan*, the Birbal stories and their counterparts, and folktales and fairytales from round the world. These resources are not easily accessible; so, anyone who wants to introduce storytelling as a regular feature of the curriculum must ensure access to a selection of stories from these resources.

What Makes a Story Good for Telling?

If we want to know the characteristics of a good story, we cannot do better than to take a story children have enjoyed listening to for generations. The *Panchatantra* story of the lion and the rabbit is a fine example. The storyline is not as simple as one might assume on account of familiarity. Let us recall its main turning points. The day comes when the little rabbit must present himself before the old lion. By the time the rabbit shows up on the lion's doorstep, the lion is mad with hunger. In this critical moment, which is obviously unsuitable for any negotiation since the lion is so, so angry, the rabbit presents his case. How did he get so late? His story of meeting another lion on the way is, of course, totally untrue, but it evokes a response in the hungry and angry lion's royal mind. He now wants to settle his rival first, and so he goes with the rabbit to inspect the well where the rival lion supposedly lives. In this crucial moment, again, the rabbit depends on his ability to carry on with his bluff and on the mindless rage and jealousy he has aroused in the lion. On seeing his own image in the well the lion cannot take it any more and jumps to his death.

Let us examine this old familiar story a little closely. For one thing, there is nothing trivial about its theme. Rather, it is about grave issues such as survival in the face of brute power and the threat of certain death. Normally we keep such issues out of our conversation with children, but apparently children have great interest in such issues. We may ask ourselves why, but I will come to that in a moment. Let me consider another important feature in the meantime. The story presents a small creature facing a crisis caused by a big, powerful creature. In order to survive the crisis, the small fellow uses a tactic which we normally consider immoral. During the course of applying this tactic, he displays some fine qualities of personality, such as courage and confidence in the face of danger, maintaining one's nerve right up to the end of a situation, and speaking to a powerful senior in socially approved ways. We must also notice the pace at which things move. The beginning establishes a strange kind of normalcy under which one animal is supposed to volunteer each day as food for the old king. Soon after this ominous routine is established, the little rabbit's turn comes, and the core of the story reveals itself. The rest of the incidents occur fast, for the rabbit cannot afford to lose a moment once he has taken the plunge into his dangerous strategy of survival. The listener is pushed from one situation to the next by means of dialogue, and it is quite clear that the listener of the story has no choice but to see everything from the rabbit's point of view.

This brief analysis should suffice to indicate some reasons for the immense popularity of this story with children. To begin with, it gives them a character or hero with whom they can fully identify. This character is the rabbit whose role in the story shares many of the predicaments and challenges that children face in their daily lives. He is small and powerless; he is required to do what he does not want to do; he is scared of dying at the hands of somebody who has total authority as well as physical force. These aspects of the rabbit's condition in the story have close parallels in every child's life although we seldom notice them, busy as we are playing our roles as parents and teachers. Few of us know, for example, that sudden death is one of the biggest sources of anxiety in childhood; so is the prospect of being in a confrontation with someone big and strong.

The story draws children's attention as soon as it begins because children can see themselves in it.[1] And then, what happens in it reinforces this attraction. The little rabbit chooses a strategy and it works. It not only works; it settles the problem forever, and for everyone. Now that is the kind of solution little children crave. The strategy also has an attraction for them because it is based on the innocent desire they always carry which is to give an excuse. The rabbit's excuse for getting late has an extra element of fascination, for it is designed not just to save his own life, but also to kill the lion. Indeed, the rabbit's predicament is so dire precisely because he cannot save himself without destroying his oppressor. So the story presents to its audience a great drama of survival by means of bravely carried out destruction. The only morality involved in it is the morality of self-survival. That too is something we cannot appreciate unless we perceive the story purely from the child's point of view. If we insist on seeing the story from an adult viewpoint, we are likely to conclude that it is an immoral story which, of course, it is.

What is the Use?

It should be clear by now that morality has nothing to do with selecting a good story for children, at least in a direct sense. At a deeper level, the story of the rabbit and the lion has an inspiring element—it shows the advantages of staying cool while facing danger; it also shows how important it is to be thoughtful and imaginative. But these are hardly 'moral' lessons in a conventional sense. In fact, great traditional stories seldom teach conventional morality. More important for us is to recognise that moral development of the child is hardly the purpose of storytelling. The real gains of storytelling are quite different, and they can be listed as follows.

Storytelling promotes good listening: Who is a good listener? One who listens to the end. That is something we cannot say about many people. Even in formal discussions people keep interrupting, partly because they are in the habit of assuming that they know in advance what the speaker is going to say, but often because they have no patience to listen. It is not surprising that listening is now regarded not merely as a skill but as an attitude which high-level courses in management and administration find important to encourage. Storytelling promotes patient listening during the formative stage of our lives when the skill of listening and the attitude it implies towards the speaker have a good chance to become lifelong habits. It is somewhat strange that good listeners have become so rare in our country which has such an old and strong oral culture. My guess is that the neglect of storytelling during childhood has a lot to do with it. Modern

India seems to have no time to tell stories regularly to children, and the consequences are becoming apparent.

Storytelling gives training in prediction: Children want to hear the stories they like again and again. The reason is that they use their familiarity with the story to test their own growing capacity to pay attention, but in an unconscious way.[2] They enjoy the fact that during a second or third listening they can successfully predict what will happen next. The joy of a prediction coming true is precisely what story-listening offers to an experienced listener; and it is not just joy: it reinforces the child-listener's confidence in his or her ability to predict. This confidence has a seminal role to play in all-round development, especially in learning how to read which is easily the biggest challenge of the first two years at school.[3] But the ability to predict also has obvious uses in learning mathematics which works on the principle of rule-governed predictability of outcomes. Stories also have rules; it is just that these rules are of a metaphorical nature. For instance, many stories follow the rule that the small creature wins by tricking the big creature. This is what happens in the rabbit-and-lion story. As children hear more and more stories, they intuitively pick up the rules governing them, and the knowledge of these rules helps them become better predictors.

Stories extend our world: The world we carry in our heads or minds is what I am talking about.[4] Stories extend it in the sense that they enable us to relate to things—both people and situations—that we never meet in our own lives. Why bother about such people or situations, then, one may ask—it is because they are part of life. Even if we do not meet them personally, they bother us in our thoughts, especially during childhood but in a general sense throughout our lifetime. Little children, for instance, worry about bad people even if none of the people surrounding them are particularly bad. Similarly, they secretly hope that they will get a chance to meet someone who is incredibly intelligent, beautiful, and good. The desire for ideal types as well as the fear of catastrophe is a part of the psychology of childhood. Traditional stories resonate this psychology, and that is why they attract children so readily.[5] By listening to stories the pre-literate child experiences by proxy a world much wider than his or her real world. Moreover, the experience that stories provide is not chaotic; rather it places a satisfying pattern or design on a chaotic world. That pattern is deeply 'moral', but not in a conventional sense. The victim does win, but often by using some objectionable means. The lie that the rabbit told the hungry lion is an example.

Stories give meaning to words: Finally, we can see the importance of storytelling in the manner that stories affect the child's expanding repertoire of language. Words are highly personal property, and the way words enable us to name the world is also highly personal. Yet, words are also a social wealth in as much as we use words to share our experiences with others. Meanings attach to words on account of this double-faced quality of words. For example, the child knows from personal experience what it is to feel hungry, but that personal meaning also helps the child to appreciate how the lion in the story must have felt when he was hungry. The story enables the listener to slightly stretch the meaning of the word 'hungry' so as to include the lion in it. The more stories one listens to, the more one's vocabulary becomes capable of including in its orbit of meaning the experiences that others bring to us. Seen this way, stories told during childhood become precursors of reading.

Indeed, all the four points discussed above in the context of storytelling are applicable to reading as well. Children's ability to read brings into play their familiarity with the rules and structures of a language. Competence in reading is crucially dependent on the ability to predict or to make an intelligen guess. On the basis of their familiarity with the structures of a language, children try to guess what might come next in a sentence or narration. Seen this way, storytelling is highly relevant to the development of literacy skills.[6]

Beyond Use

Telling stories on a regular basis can help us achieve these goals. But, it does little justice to the heritage of storytelling to place it in this kind of instrumentalist frame of appreciation, even if our primary concern is to promote it in the present-day school system. The alternative is to appreciate storytelling for its intrinsic worth which lies in its pluralistic inheritance. Storytelling deserves to be seen as a civilisational practice which permits us to protect the diversity of cultural experiences and stances from the homogenising effects of modern education and media. Storytelling also needs to be celebrated as an oral heritage, in the obvious sense that its aesthetic merits and appeal evolved by means of oral communication and memory, as well as with reference to the oral competence that storytelling as an everyday practice calls for. It is in this wider frame of worth that we ought to identify its significance and role for young children at school.

We can distinguish storytelling as an aspect of the human heritage from the skill or craft involved in the act of telling a story. As a heritage, it forms the centre of practices which enabled extended communities to symbolically represent their distinct insights and wisdom. Stories told over time in distinct geographical regions and cultures became characteristic of those cultures. Centuries or millenia later, we can still recognise in them the images and ideas peculiar to those cultures. Thus, a native Indian story from north America stands apart from a European folktale in its theme, structure, and pacing. Not just the mapping of relationships characteristic of a society, but also its cosmology and its ways of recognising the basic challenges of life are reflected in a story that has evolved in it. When we tell the story we have chosen out of the vast repertoire of the world's story heritage, we participate in the psycho-social universe of the culture in which the story arose and acquired its popular form. Thus, by telling a story, we invoke the culture that gave it birth. And not just briefly for the duration it takes to tell the story, but in a more lasting sense as well, for the reason that a well-told story is likely to be remembered, especially if it is told several times.

Stories coming from the same cultural or geographical region may have a remarkably different texture of symbolic meanings, depending on the historical phase in the development of the culture in which they find their present-day form. Many of the *Panchatantra* stories—like the one analysed above—represent the instinct for survival, imprinted as they are by a culture in which the fear that power might be used without justice was common. The *Jataka* tales, by contrast, represent a world of relationships and meanings structured around a benign hope. Apparently they acquired their form and fame during a period of deep social and political churning in Indian society. The world represented in the *Jataka* stories, more so the world they propose, is a benign place in which the potential for transformation is so great that it keeps every situation fluid and dynamic.

Another striking difference can be seen between the anthropomorphic world of the *Panchatantra*, in which human instincts and perspectives use the mask of animal characters, and the *Jataka* world where the human, the non-human, and the non-living intermesh, representing the state of 'interbeing'.[7] Realisation, rather than retribution, is the favoured narrative solution of the *Jataka*. Cleverness does not count for much; rather, it is the will to change and to see things differently, that creates the hope of a solution to the problem posed in a story. This is obviously an altogether different moral universe from the one represented in the *Panchatantra*, though both are equally significant members of India's great story heritage. The stunning diversity of stances towards the basic questions of life we see in these and other story traditions is also a testimony to the pluralism inherent in Indian civilisation.

The scope of this discussion can be easily extended by including in it the story traditions of other cultures. Each story tradition conveys the defining impact of geography and social conditions, and also of the historical experiences a culture has undergone. This is why we are able to distinguish a French, a Scandinavian, and a Russian tale without being told about its place of origin. The notion of a monolithic Western culture disappears when we recognise the diversity of formal features and themes in European story traditions. A similar thing would happen if we subjected the popularly held concept of an Eastern or Oriental culture to a scrutiny based on the story traditions, for example, of India, China, and Japan.

The diversity of cultural content and worldviews notwithstanding, all storytelling traditions represent an oral culture of communication. In a world in which literary and electronic media dominate our concept of communication, it is hardly surprising that we rarely worry about, or show respect for, morality as culture. In a literate social universe, those who depend on oral communication are referred to, derisively, as illiterates. They are inevitably regarded as being unfortunate, even handicapped, constituting an impediment to the nation's progress. Any attempt to highlight the value of the oral is labelled as being romantic and wistful. Yet, a great deal of life continues to present challenges that can only be met orally. Listening to a story temporarily places the child in an orally organised culture. The least we can expect from this experience is that it will supplement, and provide a counterbalancing element in the child's educational growth in a literacy-dominated culture. As an organising principle, oral communication imparts immediacy and directness to human relationships, both of which are important ingredients of a democratic order. Even if universalisation of literacy seems more visibly related to equality and democratic participation under present-day circumstances, oral communication must be granted the role of creating an ethos in which egalitarian relationships might find an opportunity to develop. When stories are told and heard with pleasure and habitual attention to detail, a culture not altogether irrelevant for modern democracies is resusicated.

Notes

1. An exhaustive analysis of children's fascination for stories can be found in F. Andre Favat's *Child and Tale: The Origins of Interest* (Urbana, III: National Council of Teachers of English, 1977).
2. Joan Tough has discussed the role of talk and narration in children's development in her book, *The Development of Meaning* (London: George Allen & Unwin, 1977).
3. Though reading has been a rather fast-moving area of research—and also prone to political and economic climates—Frank Smith's *Reading* (Cambridge: Cambridge University Press, 1978) has remained a classic.
4. See James Britton, *Language and Learning* (London: Allen Lane, 1971).
5. See Bruno Bettelheim, *The Use of Enchantment* (New York: Vintage, 1977).
6. An overview of this subject can be found in Krishna Kumar, *The Child's Language and the Teacher* (New Delhi: National Book Trust, 1999).
7. The concept of 'interbeing' is of central significance in Buddhism. for an exposition, see Thich Nhat Hanh, *The Heart of the Buddha's Teaching* (New York: Broadway, 1999).

6

Growing Up Male

One way for men to relate to the condition of women and their problems is by considering how boys are brought up. Their socialisation as male children is concerned with women, not just in the sense that it involves women as mothers, sisters, and so on, but also in the more crucial sense that in order to become men they have to accept and behave according to a certain predetermined image of women.

The data I discuss below are highly local and limited, but they do offer a somewhat unconventional point of entry into the symbolic universe that shapes the male personality in our country. My data are from a small town, an ex-princely state in Madhya Pradesh. Hundreds of such descriptions would have to be acquired in order to place male socialisation in some kind of a broader perspective.

In my boyhood, the most significant event that shaped my map of the place of men and women in the world was my entry into a state-run, all-boys secondary school, after finishing the primary grades. Even at the primary school stage, co-education was extremely rare those days. The fact that my primary school allowed boys to sit with girls had something to do with the ethos of basic education.[1] Boys and girls not only sat together, they shared all craft-based activities that the school offered—

book-binding, paper designing, weaving, embroidery, cooking, and gardening.

One got so used to being with girls and to seeing them as ordinary children that it proved almost traumatic to move up to a secondary school where all children were boys and even the teachers were all men.[2] This sudden separation from girls made no sense at first; a little later it led us to see girls as an enigma; and finally, we accepted it as a protection that society offered us against the danger of coming in contact with a female human before we were ready for such contact. This rationalising took years; it was a tedious process, demanding tremendous amounts of psychic energy; and, of course, we never had access to an adult to ask any questions about the great mystery of girls and their separation from us.

Girls went to a school that was designed conspicuously differently from the boys' school. In the centre of the girls' school was a courtyard where they played in total seclusion and safety from the outside world. Despite all these years since my childhood, I can still hear the shouts of girls playing games in that courtyard—shouts that we heard from our side of a broken wall, which we often toyed with the idea of climbing over. Enclosed by a ring of classrooms, Ashok trees, and the wall, the girls' school was legally accessible through a twenty-foot high iron gate that was opened only twice a day—to let the girls in and to let them out. The boys' school had no such courtyard or major entrance. Our playground was an annexe, just a big space attached to the school, devoid of any symbolism of confinement. This architectural difference between boys' and girls' schools is an important aspect of our school culture and it has persisted to this day.

Every evening we watched those hundreds of school girls in their blue skirts walking home in silent clusters of six or seven, crowding the narrow streets of the small town in a compact, neat style. As they walked they looked impossibly purposeful. We boys used the street for so many different things—as a place to stand about watching, to run round and play, to try out the manoeuverability of our bikes. Not so for girls. As we noticed all the time, for girls the street was simply a means to get straight home from school. And even for this limited use of the street they always went in clusters, perhaps because behind their purposeful demeanour they carried the worst fears of being assaulted. Watching those silent clusters for years eroded my basic sense of endowing individuality to every human being. I got used to believing that girls were not individuals.

'By separating the sexes unnaturally for almost ten years after puberty we have invented a social system which defies all physiological, psychological, and cultural logic. It is perhaps one of the major aberrations in the history of mankind.' When Dinesh Mohan wrote this in an article on university education, it was seen as a little joke.[3] I have never come across any other reference to the separation of boys from girls as a factor which influences the culture and achievement of education in our country. To my mind it is a weightier factor than campus politics and the erosion of university autonomy combined.

The government has no specific policy guidelines on the question of co-education. Both at the secondary school and the college stage, separate institutions for girls continue to be started in the name of promoting female education. Apart from legitimising the 'purdah' system, such institutions perpetuate the tragic pattern of socialisation, of which I have offered a glimpse. I call this pattern tragic because it dehumanises. The boy who learns to perceive girls as objects annihilates his chances of relating to a woman as a friend and of enriching his life with such a relationship. He becomes a victim of his own attitudes. He begins to lead a life in which the desire for sex is transformed into the need to oppress, a point I will discuss below. Our university campuses and colleges are full of such boys.

This discussion may suggest that co-education is the answer to the problem. It may be an answer but it is by no means easy or straightforward. By merely putting boys and girls together we cannot solve the problem of stereotyping of girls by boys and by male teachers. A student of mine, Bharati Roychoudhury, studied the behaviour of male teachers in mixed classrooms in Delhi schools and concluded that girls were given far less attention, encouragement, and opportunities for responsible action than boys. In England, several educators have expressed the view that co-educational schools offer fewer opportunities to girls than all-girls schools do.[4]

Such a view does not surprise me and I find it extremely important to keep it in mind when we urge the government to move towards co-education in all schools. Unless such a move is accompanied by significant changes in teacher training, the move may end up being counter-productive to girls. I believe that stereotyping of personality on the basis of sex is just as rampantly common among school teachers as it is among other members of society. Teachers will have to be trained to deal with boys and girls in an undiscriminating way if we want to humanise the culture of our schools by making them co-educational.

Aggressiveness and the desire to appear tough, combined with and arising from a deep fear of women, were common among us by the time we came to the final years of the secondary school. Some of the boys who were older talked about marriage as an event that involved tremendous risk and adventure. We had learnt from textbooks, songs, dramas, and lectures about the great celibate saints and poets of the Bhakti period. In the lives and personal development of some of them, we thought freedom from women had played an important role. We had also read some verses written during the Riti period, and some of these, especially the ones we were supposed to read for the undergraduate course in Hindi literature, gave such precise descriptions of the female body that even our teachers felt too embarrassed to read them aloud.

To us it appeared that marriage was the only sure means to get close to a woman, and we found it very ironical and cruel that this one means was fraught with an impossible challenge and personal risk. No one seemed to know precisely what the challenge or risk was, but it was unquestioned tacit knowledge that if you did not want to be defeated by a girl you must dominate her. Boasting about one's strength was extremely common. Some of the older boys were devout worshippers of Hanuman and Shiva—in that order—and they firmly believed that these gods were especially meant for men.

In the first part of his autobiography *Kya bhooloon kya yaad karoon*, the Hindi poet Harivanshrai Bachchan describes in great detail the tremendous anxiety he went through in the months preceding his marriage. It would be wrong to dismiss the anxiety and the behaviour linked with it as a universal phenomenon or to hide them under that amorphous, handy label called 'human nature'. I think the desire to achieve 'success' in one's sexual life after marriage is a cultural configuration, and at least one of its many roots can be found in the culture of our schools and colleges.

Apart from separation of the sexes, this culture is characterised by total silence on sexual behaviour and by subtle promotion of the ideal of celibacy as a qualification of sainthood. The stereotyping of female—as well as male—characters in textbooks is just one segment of the school culture. Now when stereotyping has come under attack from everyone concerned, it has been happily replaced by cardboard characters that NCERT's writers are eminently capable of constructing and which seem to satisfy the critics. The agenda of dehumanisation of girls, and, of course, boys too (although it takes place at a different level), has entered a new phase.

The crucial part of growing up male was to learn to see girls as objects. I say 'learn' because I still remember my perception of girls before I had begun to see them as objects and that my perception then was very different from what it became later. The sources of learning were many, the most important among them being other boys. Our contact with girls was minimal, in the sense that we hardly ever talked to any girl who was not a relative. And, of course, a sister did not count as a girl. On the other hand, we saw hundreds of girls each day of our lives—girls we could never hope to talk to. We saw cinema posters and sometimes films which mostly veered around cardboard female characters. Some of us read books that verged on pornography, where the treatment of the female was like that of a lifeless object that has no capacity to either suffer or enjoy. The conversations we overheard often consisted of references to women as a problem, and some of these conversations were among women themselves. I can recall several conversations among old women referring to girls as temporary property.

Equally profound was the influence of abusive terms that many boys used all the time and even in the presence of adults, including teachers. These terms were metaphors of sexual intercourse, and the terms mostly referred to different categories of men; so, one learnt to see men as belonging to different types and levels of mettle or perdition, depending on who they had subjected to intercourse. In brief, as a boy I was surrounded by a powerful discourse that delineated girls and women as sex objects, with little or nothing of their own in life in terms of sensation or demand.

This kind of discussion leads one to wonder whether socialisation is a closed process. Such a thought is endorsed in the view that the school and community should be complementary to each other in socialising the young. If one accepts this principle of complementariness, then there is no hope of changing the prevailing code of sex-typing through education, which means that there is no hope that education can intervene in the cultural reproduction of entrenched sex roles. Yet, educationists never tire of telling the world that education is an agency of change. How does one get out of this contradiction? I think the way out is to propose counter-socialisation as the school's domain. That is, we need not see the school as an institution working in harmony with the community or the larger society in the matter of sex-role socialisation. On the contrary, we need to perceive the school in conflict with the community's code of socialisation.

This line of thought would lead us to reflect on the ways and means by which the school can act as a counter-socialiser in sex-role learning. If the community believes in segregating the sexes during adolescence, the school must set an alternative example by mixing the sexes. Similarly, while the larger social ethos offers stereotyped models of the roles of men and women, the school must insist that the adults working in it will not act in stereotyped and stereotyping ways. In the world outside the school, knowledge about sex is taboo; in the school such knowledge must be accessible.

Cinema and television cash in on conservative images of women and men; the school's media—that is, textbooks and other materials—should offer images and symbols that motivate the reader to look at human beings in terms of their own struggle for an identity, rather than as reciting prefabricated conversations. And finally, if acceptance of the prevailing order and its norms is what society demands, then the school should demand the spirit of inquiry and offer opportunities to practise it. If all this sounds an idealistic, tall order, then one must remember that the agenda of changing women's place and role in society is no different.

Notes

1. I am saying 'ethos' and not the policy of basic education. Gandhi did not believe in co-education, nor did other famous basic educators. But, the plan of basic education created an ethos in which all kinds of innovations could take place.
2. The primary school described here admitted boys till the early sixties after which it shed its 'basic' character as well as its co-educational policy. It was a government school, and in changing its policy it must have followed the directive of a local officer. The government does not have any clear-cut policy on co-education.
3. 'Virus on the campus' in *Seminar* (293, January 1984).
4. For one such discussion see *Co-education Reconsidered,* edited by Rosemary Deem (Milton Keynes: Open University Press, 1984).

7

Secularism: Its Politics and Pedagogy

Instead of dithering over the larger problem of finding a working definition of secularism in the Indian context, let us dive into the more specific problem of locating an educational correlative of secularism. In other and simpler words, our problem at hand is to decide how a secular ideology can be translated into educational practice. I am of course not interested in pursuing this problem here as a challenge for educational theory, but rather as a point of inquiry into educational history and policy. I propose to reach out for the core issue involved in this challenge by examining a passage from Jawaharlal Nehru's book, *Discovery of India*. It is a significant passage partly because it is one of the few statements made by Nehru on the conceptual issues involved in children's education. But a greater significance can be attributed to it if we notice that in this brief passage, Nehru engages in a dialogue with his eminent colleague, Gandhi. Viewed from this angle, the passage provides us with a very useful entry point into the two modes of secularism associated with these two men.

The excerpt is from the final paragraphs of a sub-chapter titled 'The Congress and Industry', from *The Discovery of India*.

> It is well recognised now that a child's education should be intimately associated with some craft or manual activity. The mind is stimulated thereby and there is a co-ordination between the activities of the mind and the hands. So also the mind of a growing boy or girl is stimulated by the machine. It grows under the machine's impact (under proper conditions, of course, and not as an exploited and unhappy worker in a factory) and opens out new horizons. Simple scientific experiments, peeps into the microscope, and an explanation of the ordinary phenomenon of nature bring excitement in their train, an understanding of some of life's processes, and a desire to experiment and find out instead of relying on set phrases and old formulae. Self-confidence and the co-operative spirit grow, and frustration, arising out of the miasmas of the past lessons. A civilisation based on ever-changing and advancing mechanical techniques leads to this. Such a civilisation is a marked change, a jump almost from the older type, and is intimately connected with modern industrialisation.[1]

There can be little doubt that while writing these words Nehru was engaging in a dialogue on 'basic education' proposed by Gandhi in 1937.[2] He starts by agreeing with the main pedagogical assumption underlying Gandhi's proposed plan that a craft or manual activity stimulates the child's mind. Then, by the force of analogy between craft and machine, he goes off on an argument that challenges the main economic assumption underlying 'basic education' without identifying or naming it. The dialogue with Gandhi's proposal that he had started, turns after two sentences into a statement regarding the pedagogical value of scientific experiments and the relation such experiments have with an industrial civilisation. Nehru was of course correct in pointing out this relationship, and also in stressing the enormous role that an experiment-based pedagogy of science could play in the revitalisation of Indian society. He was apparently in agreement with many Indian modernist intellectuals who found Gandhi's educational plan uninviting, and in some cases unacceptable. Nehru's response to Gandhi's plan is subtly expressed when after acknowledging that manual activity stimulates the child's mind, he says, 'So also the mind of a growing boy or girl is stimulated by the machine'. In the rest of the passage he builds on this function of the machine, telling us about the role that microscopes can play in schools and in children's lives.

Rival Worldviews

Among the people responding to Gandhi's proposal were many who felt no need to be as subtle as Nehru, and who found Gandhi's educational plan a source of irritation, a digression worth avoiding. For example, Mulk Raj Anand wrote that basic education would only turn 'good little minds' into 'morons' who would 'vegetate within the limits of their self-sufficient communities'.[3] In one metaphorical stroke, Anand gives us the alternative of Nehru's dream of a civilisation based on industrialisation and the scientific temper as opposed to the narrow, enclosed world of the Indian village. Anand's response to 'basic education' was by no means unique. The joint secretary in the education department, G.S. Bajpai, confessed in a personal communication to V.S.S. Sastri: 'I am no lover of the "Wardha" stunt as you call it. One object we had in persuading the Central Advisory Board of Education to appoint a committee to go into the Wardha scheme was to provide an opportunity for authoritative exposure of its crudities and absurdities.'[4] If we prepared a Venn diagram to classify reactions to Gandhi's basic education proposal, we would place these articulate rejections within the boundary that would also include Nehru's highly guarded reaction. It is hardly surprising that the National Planning Committee, of which Nehru was the chairman, saw the basic education scheme as a digression. The NPC's sub-committee on education argued that there had been since 1938 a sudden increase in the efficiency of primary schools under the Congress ministries (the data given in support of this claim were confined to Bombay), and 'it would, therefore, be wrong to displace the movement by one in favour of basic education'.[5] The sub-committee also found the excessive emphasis given in basic education on productive skills unacceptable. Its report said that the stress on such skills will be 'spiritually harmful' and 'will mean existence of child labour in schools.'

The rival worldviews underlying our Venn can be projected by two symbols: the microscope and the *charkha*. Both were machines, but machines of a different status, and presenting two different kinds of political economies. The microscope symbolised a modern, industrial economy and a society controlled by a state whose legitimacy extended to its cultural projections. Such a state was the primary instrument to shape people's consciousness. Those who believed in such a state perceived independent India's major challenge as being one of modernisation of its economic base by rapid industrialisation; the rest—which included the maturation of a secular society—would follow. From the rival perspective, the one symbolised by the charkha, the major challenge for Indian society was inequality. The political economy of the charkha and its pedagogy was to aim at enhancing the stamina and power of the oppressed masses *before* the arrival of advanced tools of production. Egalitarian and communitarian values had to be promoted first; the march of industrialisation could wait. In this model too, the state had a crucial role to perform—to delay the advancement of modern tools of production. Where was the class to sustain this ideological state? This is the key question we ought to ask in order to probe the civilisational agenda of Gandhi's plan. On the other side of our Venn, the relevant question for us to ask is, 'Where were the microscopes to give millions of school children a peep?'

Pedagogical Failure

From a pedagogical perspective, both the charkha and the microscope appear equally worthy as symbols of a secular epistemology for schools. Both of them promise to mediate between the teacher and the child, and to mitigate the supreme authority that Brahminical traditions endow upon the teacher.[6] To the extent that this kind of authority is responsible for stultifying the child's desire to ask and pursue questions, the two symbols offer the same autonomy to children. No doubt, there is an enormous gap between the availability of microscopes or charkhas in classrooms, and the vision of a classroom in which children are learning on their own initiative. This gap calls for hard work by well-trained and motivated teachers. There is no guarantee that microscopes or charkhas by themselves will open up the possibility of child-centred learning, but the point here is that both the symbols represent a precondition for the establishment of secular epistemology in schools. In the context of pedagogy, secularism implies, among several other things, the possibility to learn from one's own actions or experience (e.g., the peep into the microscope or the feel of the thread one has woven) rather than from the word of someone in authority. Such a possibility cannot arise in schools where children have nothing to touch, manipulate or work with, where the teacher and the prescribed text are the only available resources for learning.

It is precisely such schools that independent India inherited. Nehru's government made no dent in the bareness and desolation of the average primary school. The only schools (in the state sector) where children got access to some objects they could work with were 'basic' schools, and their privileged position in this regard had a short life. Once 'basic' education ceased to have even the token significance it had acquired in the fifties, school learning went squarely back to where it had been—to dependence on the teacher's word and the prescribed textbook.

The temporary pedagogical base provided by 'basic' education for secular learning was decimated by the mid-sixties. The charkha was too outmoded a tool for the Education Commission, which did its work during the peak years of the so-called 'development decade' and the Green Revolution. The commission reiterated the *etatiste* elite's belief in the scientific temper and the cultural implication of industrialisation, but the supply of microscopes to schools was another matter. They figured nowhere in the state's policy on education. We are of course referring to microscopes as a symbol of the state's interest in modernising the school system.

It is against this background that educational theory enjoins us to view the frustration that many secularists have expressed over recent years. They feel that secularism has taken a beating. There are, of course, many signs indicating this, the rise of religious revivalism being one. Some of them are now willing to suggest that secularism was not quite appropriate for India in the first place. Others want it to be defined differently. And still others want the fight for secularism to continue despite the damp weather prevailing today. From an educational perspective, this stance looks somewhat bizarre. If we can assume that education is a prime instrument for constructing a social base for secularism, then the question one asks in order to assess the performance of secularist ideology since Independence is: 'Were any credible efforts made to provide for secular pedagogy?' If the answer is a clear 'no', what is there to feel frustrated or defeated about? In a different context, Amartya Sen suggests that the relevant question for us to ask is: 'How can you reap what you did not sow'?[7]

A credible attempt to use education as an agency of socialisation and training in secular thought was never made. Instead an attempt was made to use education as a means to propagate secularism. The difference between the two approaches is vital. The approach that was tried in our country involved little concern for modernising the education system by changing its inner works, such as the decision-making processes in curriculum, teacher training, and the teacher's professional autonomy. These inner works of our system carry the codes of Brahminical traditions of pedagogy, and some codes of power relations in a colonial society.[8] They were of course not designed to socialise children in secular thought and attitudes. The Brahminical codes of teacher-pupil relations had their function in a quasi-feudal order sustained by a primarily agricultural society. The codes concerning the teacher's professional role and status developed during the colonial period when the power to project valid forms of knowledge was deposited in the bureaucratic apparatus of the state. Neither of the two kinds of codes permitted inquiry as a mode of learning. This is what made the education system a very poor agency of secular thought and values.

The state of independent India did not pay much attention to developing new capacities in the agency. It forged ahead to propagate secularism as an explicit message. To a certain extent, the state was guided by the belief that education per se was an instrument of modernisation and would therefore spread secular values. At the same time, the state went ahead to use the medium of textbooks—the only kind of school literature that exists in our system—to project secular ideals.

Rewriting of History

Among school subjects, civics was apparently the most convenient one to provide the content for explicit projection of state ideals, including the ideal of secularism. History came next, and despite obstacles, the state—at any rate, the state apparatus at the level of the central government—succeeded in using school history to propagate secular values. The involvement of well-known left-wing historians such as Bipan Chandra, Romila Thapar, and R.S. Sharma in the preparation of school history books published by the National Council of Educational Research and Training, continues to be a major testimony of the state's sincerity in pursuing its aim of propagating secularism. As a political accomplishment, the rewriting of history has been widely appreciated. It has been seen as a triumph of the cultural policy normally associated with Nehru's own outlook and political vision.

As far as the rewriting of history as a political statement goes, the NCERT's history books undoubtedly made a clear political statement. The clarity of this statement was proved when these books came under a cloud during the period of the Janata Party's government. Hindu revivalist elements with the Janata Party made a concerted attempt to usurp NCERT's history programme.[9] It is easy to see the failure of this attempt as evidence of the tenacity of Nehru's legacy in building the ideology of the Indian state. On the other hand, if the attempt had succeeded, we would have seen the fragility of the state-centred policy of decision-making in curriculum. Indeed, this fragility can surface any time, and the day may not be far when Hindu revivalism may come to dominate the state apparatus for education. As we know too well by now, revivalism is no more a party creed confined to any particular organisation in the spectrum of mass politics.

But we need not wait for the fragility of curriculum decision-making to prove itself. A visit to a classroom where the NCERT's history is being taught will provide sufficient proof to show the naivete of the belief that secular textbooks mean socialisation in secularism. What we discover in classrooms is that the ideological character of these textbooks does not affect the pedagogical relations entrenched in the schools as a social institution. As we have noted, the entrenched pedagogical relations allot to the learner the role of a mute, unquestioning receiver. This role militates against the very basis of the secular ideal of questioning. In the West, secularism implied the individual's right to question the explanatory powers of religious authority. In the Indian context, the explanatory powers of religion do not function via the mediating agency of an established clergy. Our tradition worked by lodging quasi-religious bits of an authority in numerous apparatuses which assisted in maintaining the socio-cultural order. Education was one such apparatus, and it served the social order by endowing upon the teacher and the given text the supreme authority to feed the young learner with legitimate truth. The learner did not need to know, in a cognitive sense, what the truth was; he only needed to accept it and reproduce it on occasions demanding the proof of his initiation into socially accepted truth. As long as learning at school remains tied to this ideal of the learner's behaviour, it hardly matters which version of history is taught through the prescribed textbook.

The point is to recognise secularism as more than ideology or a message to be passed round. In the context of education, it is an implicit product of modern pedagogical practices that we associate with Rousseau's tradition. In the twentieth century this tradition has found unmistakable support in the findings of Piaget's genetic epistemology. Pioneers of modern pedagogy invented and argued for ways to place the learner at the centre of education. They emphasised the importance of the individual child as a unit of the teacher's attention. They provided the fuel with which the battle for enhancement of public funds for education could be fought. In the chain of their logic, respect and provision for the individual child's initiative and inquiry was the key value. This value is the essence of the secular temper we talk about and hope to disseminate in our bare primary schools with the help of poorly paid, bureaucratically enslaved teachers.

Ideological Tool

From this perspective, dissemination of secularism through education works like one of the many dreams professed by the Indian bourgeois classes and their leaders after Independence. Before it became a dream, it had begun to serve as a behavioural attribute, a gleaming virtue to wear. In the constellation of values that the Indian bourgeois leadership in the final years of the Independence struggle came to be associated with, indifference to religion in public life had acquired a prominent position. Its political importance lay in providing a counter to the demand for Pakistan. Its social importance, and that interests us more in the context of education, lay in providing a symbol of distinction between the educated person and the masses. While the educated person was supposed to be indifferent to religion, at least in public, the masses were regarded as being steeped in religious consciousness and rituals. Secularism became a cover for the educated person to hide his secret dependence on the psychic securities that religion provided. Education became a mask which he wore in public, to profess his preference for scientific explanations for life's big questions and to claim intellectual superiority over the 'ignorant' millions.

The usefulness of secularism as an ideological tool in the hands of the bourgeois can now be fully appreciated. The immediacy of its political use, and its significance as one of the determinants of status were but steps towards its ultimate usefulness as a class ideology. This ultimate use lay in its capacity to mystify the material base of a secular outlook. This mystification was accomplished by the projection of the secular outlook as a product of education, and by the corresponding projection of obscurantism as a product of illiteracy. These projections concealed the significant role that a change in basic material conditions affecting human life and health plays in promoting secular attitudes.

From this perspective, willingness to accept and to act on secular explanations requires certain basic securities which are historically linked with scientific and industrial revolutions and the rise of the welfare state. Prevention of sudden, premature death on a large scale, and the availability of support systems that promised reasonably dependable standards of longevity and health had a great deal to do with the dilution of other-worldly, religious or quasi-religious beliefs concerning life and death. In the industralised countries of Europe, a secular worldview did not depend on propaganda campaigns against religiosity; indeed the spirit of religion never died in these countries, nor did the scientific temper become a mass, or even an elite religion. All that happened was that the function of religion as a source of explanation for unhappiness, death, disease, and poverty diminished, without much diminution in the function of religion as a source of solace. When child mortality declined, and it became possible to expect reasonable health in old age, secular explanations of poverty and disease gained ground.

In India, the advocates of secularism by and large ignored this linkage. They professed secularism as an ideology. They hoped that the state could actually propagate secularism with the help of education and the media, even as the majority of deaths continued to occur in childhood, and life for the poor remained totally unpredictable and tenuous. This was obviously a fond hope, and it is little wonder that secularism has not made impressive strides along the route the Indian bourgeois had charted for it. The failure of secularism is hardly the failure of an ideology. It is essentially the failure of a ruling class that used secular ideals as a means of seeking legitimacy, but which largely ignored the social tasks associated with the development of a secular society.

Many observers of contemporary India succumb to the urge to explain away the decline of secularism in terms of a mismatch between secularism as a Western credo and Indian culture.[10] What validity such explanations have is hard to judge by any objective standards, if only because the naming or characterisation of a culture is itself a political act. We end up in the terrain of rhetoric and its social uses if we agree to discuss the nature of the Indian culture or psyche as a variable affecting the fate of secularism. We need not enter that terrain as long as a quotidian social act like delivering a baby continues to pose each day a risk to the lives of thousands of women and as long as about half the deaths occurring in the nation are those of children below six. Let the welfare state first make motherhood and childhood reasonably safe. Let the state modernise elementary-level pedagogy to the extent that every child can touch, smell, observe, and think at school. If obscurantist beliefs and practices still continue to hold sway, we shall have defensible reason to talk about the nature of Indian culture and things of that sort. It is good to remember that real advancements in mass health and education cannot be made in the absence of a serious disturbance in the relationship patterns that determine access to power and its exercise. This is why it is correct to claim that 'it is not the expansion of knowledge that is so crucial, as the expansion of popular power' for the growth of a secular temper in society.[11]

Notes

1. Jawaharlal Nehru, *The Discovery of India* (London: Meridian, 1960) first published, 1946; 416.
2. *The Discovery of India* was written in Ahmednagar Fort prison between April and September, 1944.
3. Mulk Raj Anand, *On Education* (Bombay: Hind Kitab, 1947): 20.
4. Letter written by G.S. Bajpai to V.S.S. Sastri, 2 May 1938, Srinivasa Sastri papers, Nehru Memorial Museum and Library, New Delhi.
5. National Planning Committee Series, Reports of Sub-Committees, *General Education and Technical Education and Developmental Research* (Bombay: Vora, 1948): 58.
6. For further discussion of this aspect, see my *Political Agenda of Education* (New Delhi: Sage, 1991).
7. This reference is to Amartya Sen's Harvard lecture delivered at New Delhi in January 1988 and excerpted in *Future*, 22–23 (Winter 87–88).
8. For further discussion along this line, see my 'Colonial Citizen as an Educational Ideal', in *Economic and Political Weekly* (28 January 1989): PE-45–51.
9. See L.I. Rudolph and S.H. Rudolph, 'Rethinking Secularism: Genesis and Implications of the Textbook Controversy, 1977–79' *Pacific Affairs*, 56:1 (Spring 1983): 1537.
10. One significant articulation of this kind is T.N. Madan's 'Secularism in Its Place', *The Journal of Asian Studies* (November 1987): 747–59.
11. S. Khan, 'Towards a Marxist Understanding of Secularism', *Economic and Political Weekly* (7 March 1987): 406–409.

8

Peace with the Past

The most obvious thing about the past is that it is past and immutable. No remarkable wisdom is required to notice this, yet it is difficult—especially in modern, literate societies—to overcome the temptation to live in the past. The construction and institutionalisation of a national memory of the past necessarily implies imparting to the past a chronic half-life. Modern systems of mass education serve as prime instruments of this process. What kind of half-life the past will have—leaky or self-contained—depends on the quality of the system of education. A leaky half-life suggests the availability of the past as a resource for evoking passions and nostalgia. In the metaphor of radioactive waste I am using, 'self-contained' knowledge of the past would mean that it is accompanied by the awareness that the past is past.

My recently published study (*Prejudice and Pride*, 2001, Penguin) of school textbooks used for the teaching of history in contemporary India and Pakistan shows that both countries transmit the knowledge of the past in a highly 'leaky' manner. This finding can hardly surprise anyone, given the backward and inefficient systems of education in both India and in Pakistan, and also in view of the low priority they attach to school-level teaching of social sciences in general and history in particular.

In both the systems of education, the teaching of history is perceived primarily as a means of citizenship training for nation-building. Although this perception is not unique to India and Pakistan, the extent to which it influences the pedagogy of social sciences, especially history, is quite remarkable, in the sense that the nation-building role of history leaves no room *whatsoever* for pedagogic objectives, such as inculcating curiosity about the past and imparting intellectual skills to make sense of it.[1] The pedagogic poverty of Indian and Pakistani textbooks becomes all the more influential, given the dominant role and recall-oriented character of the examination system and its linkages with the prescribed textbook.

My clubbing of India and Pakistan in the preceding paragraph may hurt many readers, and I can fully empathise with them. As educated Indians, we have all been socialised to perceive the creation of Pakistan as an act of betrayal and narrow-mindedness; and now, more than half a century later, we are led to believe that Pakistan is a failed state. While comparing ourselves to Pakistan, we take pride in having survived so far as a democracy, and especially as a secular democracy. These assumed points of our superiority are grounded in the contours of our knowledge of history, particularly our knowledge of Partition and the decade preceding it.

School textbooks offer us a valuable means of analysing this common knowledge, bits and pieces of which are dispersed by the Indian and the Pakistani systems of education within their respective territories. My study of a sample of these textbooks reveals that they socialise children into the ideological perspectives of two master narratives.[2] The clashing structures of the two master narratives explain why India and Pakistan perceive themselves as irreconcilable to each other though they have been in existence as separate nation-states for more than fifty years now.

The Indian master narrative is structured round the idea that secular nationalism and communalism were historically alien to each other, and that the former is politically and morally superior. In the binary that Indian textbooks use to narrate the story of Independence, secular nationalism symbolises an accommodative, rationally organised vision of social transformation, while communalism symbolises regressive social forces, seeking sustenance from primordial sources of inspiration, including religion.

The Pakistani master narrative denies that India's struggle for independence was secular. At the heart of this narrative lies the two-nation theory which claims that the urge to create Pakistan arose out of certain irreconcilable differences between Hindus and Muslims. The Indian narrative, of course, denies the validity of this theory, and by doing so, it disapproves of Pakistan' imbuing its existence—as the signifier of a regressive, divisive tendency— with suspicion. The structural features of the two master narratives I have outlined above impose severe pedagogic restrictions on them. These restrictions pertain to what the narratives can include as relevant historical facts or happenings and, also, to how the course of the happenings selected for mention or emphasis should be paced. These are among the features or symptoms which enable us to analyse the two master narratives in a comparative manner.

For instance, the secular/communal binary which the Indian school histories use to tell the story of freedom does not allow them to acknowledge that there were organisational and social overlaps between the two ideologies. That Hindu communalism had a substantial presence in the Congress, and that it exercised great influence on the political and cultural ethos of the thirties remain unmentionable for many Indian text writers, and those who mention them do not attach any crucial significance to these facts. Apparently, any emphasis on Hindu communalism, especially on its role within the Congress, would spoil the neatness of the secular/communal binary which gives the Indian master narrative a basic structure and also a moral overtone.

Simplistic separation of the secular from the communal outlook also affects the school historian's ability to use biography—an important aspect of the learning of history during childhood—in a purposive and credible manner. All eminent leaders of the freedom struggle end up becoming examples of a homogeneous bag of values. History textbooks fail to show why, for example, Tilak, Gokhale, Lajpat Rai, Bose, Nehru, and Gandhi must be regarded as distinct personalities and political figures. An undifferentiating label of greatness that these and others carry defeats any larger intellectual purpose that the inclusion of history in the school syllabus might serve. The much avowed inspirational role of history becomes a mere shell when any analytical details that might help children perceive great personalities as leaders engaged in a political struggle are withdrawn.

History turns into a brochure, and the personalities involved in it become cardboard figures juggled around in the theatre of significant events. That applies to Gandhi and Jinnah in both Indian and Pakistani textbooks, especially towards the closing scenes of their respective narratives. Some lives are sliced into two halves, one acceptable to the Indian textbook writers, and the other to their Pakistani counterparts. This is the fate of Syed Ahmad Khan and Iqbal.

Basically, both countries treat the history of the freedom struggle as a moral tale. The Indian version highlights the triumph of secular nationalism, and the Pakistani version shows how a cultural vision was realised despite gigantic political obstacles. Neither version has the capacity to accommodate complexities and ambiguities. The Indian version virtually forgets about Muslim politics after the hopes born during the short Congress-League collaboration over Khilafat had died. From here onwards, the narrative must avoid the news of all but pro-Congress Muslims; that is why the Nehru Report, the meagre participation of Muslims in the Civil Disobedience Movement, the discord over basic education during the late 1930s, and the Lahore Resolution are glossed over.

The Pakistani textbooks give the Nehru Report a key place in the story they present; even the most compressed accounts find room for Jinnah's fourteen points. The controversy surrounding Gandhi's proposal for basic education also gets elaborate attention. But then, the brush with which both these matters are portrayed is too thick to do justice to the ideological struggle that existed within the Congress. Our ignoring Hindu revivalist influence on the Congress enables the Pakistani school historian to target the Congress more purposefully—in terms of the larger orbit of meaning which Pakistan's young citizens are supposed to inhabit psychologically—by calling it a Hindu organisation committed to establishing Hindu *raj* in India.

Of course, one can appreciate why the Indian narrative pays little attention to the course of post-1920s Muslim politics. The obvious reason is that the sub-plot of Muslim politics now onwards belongs to the story of Pakistan's freedom, not India's. However, our appreciation of this simple nationalistic logic should not blind us to the pedagogic, and equally significantly, the political cost of the school historian's decision.

The pedagogic cost is that the 1940s must come as a surprise. Without the background of the social and political alienation of the Muslim landed elite and the intelligentsia of the northern plains, the student can hardly make sense of the sudden emergence of the Muslim League as a powerful actor during the early 1940s. Not surprisingly, the Indian narrative becomes extremely reluctant to go into the details of any event following the Quit India Movement. Textbooks jump from one mention to the next, rushing towards Partition, which, from the point of view of the young student, begs for an explanation more substantial than what the British-Muslim conspiracy theory can provide.

The subjectivity of millions, as shaped by the socialisation inherent in the fable of freedom, sustains the South Asian geopolitical order. By depriving children of any rational means to comprehend the overlap between secular and communal nationalisms, the Indian narrative of the national movement socialises the young to perceive Pakistan as an illegitimate achievement. The rival persuasion, to which the Pakistani narrative is educated—both as a matter of educational policy and the structure of the story—is to see India as a Hindu nation. The denial of India's claim of being a secular state is central to the 'Pakistan Ideology' that school textbooks are supposed to uphold and disseminate.[3] It requires either complete avoidance or, in the case of steadier accounts, serious downplaying of any events and personalities marking the spirit of secular nationalism which opposed Partition on moral grounds though it could not stop it from becoming a political reality.

Between 1857 and 1947, we can find episodes where the two narratives converge and others where they diverge. In Partition, we find symptoms of both kinds. The two narratives come remarkably close in the cursory manner in which they deal with the violence associated with Partition. The horror and suffering that millions of ordinary men and women faced receive no more than a few lines of cold recording in most Indian and Pakistani textbooks. But, the treatment of Partition as a political event is completely different in the two narratives. For the Indian textbook writers, it was a terrible tragedy that marred the glory of Independence. For the Pakistani textbook writers, it was a stunning achievement, marking an escape for the Muslims from the impending Hindu raj.

By giving Partition the status of a great political—and not just human—tragedy, the Indian narrative fuses the secular and the communal perspectives which had so far stayed altogether separate from each other. Partition evokes an irreparable sense of national loss and victimisation in both progressive and conservative varieties of school historiography. The division of India becomes a memory that Indians must forever regret.

In turn, the Muslims who share the blame for this act with the British in divided India's national record must continue to serve as a stereotype of betrayer. No wonder, the word 'Pakistan' is used as the name of a tendency in cinema and literature; and whenever communal violence recurs, the memory of the creation of Pakistan is inevitably invoked. It is also not surprising that when a visitor from Pakistan talks about peace, substantial parts of the audience slip into the fantasy of a future when the two nations will be reunited. The visitor is mystified to think why his learned Indian listeners don't realise that reuniting with India will mean death for Pakistan and its struggle to establish a separate national identity.

The Pakistani portrayal of Partition as an apolitical event also suffers from a sense of irony. The uncertainty and anguish that Jinnah went through at the time of Partition cannot be represented, for it would diminish the superhuman image that school textbooks give him. Textbook writers also find it hard to reconcile the idea of the formation of Pakistan as preordained by destiny with that of being one of active participation to effect its actual birth. The Pakistani master narrative alludes to the two-nation theory soon after its coverage of the 1857 revolt, citing Syed Ahmad Khan as its earliest proponent. By the time the narrative reaches the early 1940s, it has already used the theory a few times to convey a sense of inevitability about the eventual creation of Pakistan.

So strongly and repeatedly does the narrative, in most textbook versions, refer to Pakistan as a goal recognised from the beginning of the freedom struggle, that the only curiosity it can satisfy in the final episode is about how the goal was ultimately attained. Yet, when it comes, the final episode conveys the message that Pakistan was the outcome of Hindu intransigence expressed in the unaccommodative attitude of the Congress.

For Indian children, not just the narrative of the freedom struggle, but history itself comes to an end with Partition and Independence. As a constituent of social studies, and later on as a subject in its own right, history runs out of content in 1947, except for some of the events associated with Independence, such as Gandhi's assassination, making of the Constitution, and the beginning of Five-Year Plans. All that has happened during the last 55 years may filter through the measly civics syllabus, popular cinema and television; history as formally constituted knowledge of the past does not cover it.

Partition remains the last major event to have 'occurred' in India's long history, and as such it can be expected to maintain in the child's mind an evocative freshness—both as an item signifying the end of the freedom struggle and as a factor of children's socialisation into a political legacy. Pakistan is a part of that legacy, and it is a highly significant political fact of contemporary South Asia that the last news Indian children get of Pakistan in the course of their institutionalised education is about its birth. For any more recent news they must depend on films like *Border* and *Ghaddar*.

For Pakistani textbooks, Partition marks neither an ending nor a discontinuity, and the narrative smoothly moves on. In the post-independence history of Pakistan, India figures quite often—in the stories of wars, in the context of Kashmir, or simply as a Hindu neighbour. Not just the teaching of history, the entire curriculum is embedded in a masculine, war-oriented and anti-Hindu ideal of the nation-state.[4] Textbooks interchange the word 'Bharat' with 'India' in a seemingly unpatterned manner, but if one looks carefully, the former gets preference in contexts which are explicitly hostile.

If J. Krishnamurty's view that modern education constitutes a major threat to world peace needed any proof, India and

Pakistan provide it in their daily teaching of history to the young.[5] So long as they continue to resist the maturity that comes from feeling at peace with the past, they will keep on wasting incalculable psychic and physical resources in the name of security. This is no familiar plea by a peace-loving dove for cutting down the defence budget, for there is no room for such a plea in a democracy grounded in public illiteracy and poor-quality education. For now, a plea for designing education, especially history, differently should suffice. That includes taking both education and history seriously.

Notes

1. For a quick introduction to the many ways in which nation-states around the world use history to inculcate pride and hatred, see 'Nations and their Past: The Uses and Abuses of History', in *The Economist* (21 December 1996): 73–76.
2. The sample included 10 textbooks from India (state textbooks of UP, Tamil Nadu, Punjab, the NCERT, and a few textbooks published by private publishers) and 8 from Pakistan (including Punjab Board textbooks and the ones published by private publishers). For titles and other details, see my *Prejudice and Pride* (New Delhi: Penguin, 2001).
3. For an introduction to the recent historical developments in Pakistan, see Ayesha Jalal, *Democracy and Authoritarianism in South Asia* (Lahore: Sang-e-meel, 1995).
4. In an earlier book, *Learning from Conflict* (New Delhi: Orient Longman, 1996), I have discussed the problems that secular-minded textbook writing faces while narrating Gandhi's assassination.
5. For a gender perspective on the teaching of social sciences in Pakistan, see Rubina Saigol, *Knowledge and Identity* (Lahore: ASR, 1995).
6. J. Krishnamurti's talk, 'Education and World Peace' in *Education and the Significance of Life* (Chennai: Krishnamurti Foundation India, 1992) is among the many pieces where this point is emphatically made.

9

Listening to Gandhi

In the new millennium many ideas practised and preached by Mahatama Gandhi are becoming increasingly relevant as guides to state policy. The most interesting, and understandably controversial, of his favourite ideas is that of local self-reliance.

In a world said to have become interdependent, local self-reliance seems irrelevant, indeed heretical. Yet the fact remains that the world is not really interdependent. Many countries of the South are caught in a debt trap which forces them to part with a substantial portion of their national income to pay the interest they owe the North. This ghastly compulsion impoverishes these countries further, rendering their labour force and natural resources steadily more vulnerable. In the so-called global village, the real village is dependent on the city for such essential needs of life as work and health care. Gandhi's insistence on local self-reliance was precisely in such basic aspects of life. The world is armed today with sophisticated technological solutions to every human problem, yet the majority of people suffer from malnutrition, unemployment, and chronic illness. This obvious contradiction suggests that Gandhi's plea for local self-reliance in the matter of basic needs deserves to be heard again.

A second salient feature of Gandhi's legacy is the importance of imaginative action. If there is such a thing as a Gandhian theory, surely it is a theory of action which emphasises role-playing with earnestness and imagination. All of Gandhi's major political and social battles, starting with his work in South Africa, illustrate this point. In retrospect, these battles seem crafted to perfection as localised socio-dramas with a universal appeal. The Salt Satyagraha is probably the best known example of such a battle, but numerous smaller episodes occurred throughout Gandhi's life. For example, when the engine installed for running the press at Phoenix Farm in South Africa failed, Gandhi successfully mobilised his colleagues to run the press manually all night so that the *Indian Opinion* would come out on time. This early event suggests two other aspects of Gandhi's theory of action, apart from commitment to one's role. One is his insistence on autonomy which translates into freedom from dependence on any single option. The other is persistence. If one looks at Gandhi's life from a pedagogical perspective, one can aptly describe it as a long lesson in the value of the freedom of initiative and tenacity to the cause at hand.

Finally, Gandhi's legacy must remind us of the significance of the spatial community and the family. Child welfare—indeed, all human welfare—has its locus in these two units of collective life in Gandhi's picture of the world. Democracy, both as a system of .governance and as a way of living, depends on the expression it finds in these two units. As Marjorie Sykes, probably the best commentator on Gandhi's educational thought, reminded a symposium a few years back, Gandhi's ideas of democratic living depends on the possibility of a face-to-face dialogue among the members of a community.[1] This ideal is of course ancient, having been established by the Greek philosophers, but its meaning and potential are yet to be realised in our age, even though our world seems to have espoused democracy as the only worthwhile form of government.

In his last book, *The Public and Its Problems* (1927), John Dewey, whose educational theory meets Gandhi's proposal or many crucial counts, talked about the difficulties that the twentieth century was facing in letting the spatial community stay alive and relevant to human life.[2] During the last decade or so, many nation-states have woken up to the damage that modern planning of societies has done to local communities and the family, leaving the child to be cared for by the faceless state. As we plan redress, we can find an important resource of ideas and inspiration in Gandhi's legacy.

The model of children's education that flows from Gandhi's vision of a desirable society strikingly matches the most important implications that one might draw from modern child psychology for organising or reforming the system of education. These implications can be listed in the following manner:

- the child's immediate milieu must serve as a resource for the rediscovery of accepted knowledge;
- children must have the freedom to create their own models of knowledge about the world;
- learning must provide for opportunities for children to be physically active; and
- classroom activities must resonate and extend the child's life at home and in its surroundings.

Gandhi's choice of the local as the appropriate context for the exercise of initiative and persistence suggests an obvious parallel to the concepts of exploration and reconstruction we find in Piaget's psycho-philosophy of knowledge. Parallels can also be drawn between the links that Dewey perceived between children's learning of subject matter and their milieu on the one hand, and Gandhi's view of the school as an institutionalised forum of the community on the other.

These parallels were reflected in the proposal Gandhi made in the specific context of education, but the proposal had another item which was related to his economics and his own early experience of teaching children at Phoenix and Tolstoy Farms in South Africa. This concerned the introduction of handicrafts as an organising principle of the school curriculum. Much has been written on this aspect of Gandhi's *nai talim* or 'new education' which is also known as 'basic education'. In summary, the idea of traditional handicrafts providing an axis for the school's daily curriculum had in it the following elements which formed its rationale:

- bridging the school with the world of work;
- imparting an activity orientation to the curriculum; and
- inculcating a sense of self-reliance.

Historical documents concerning the attempt made between the late thirties and the late fifties to give a 'basic' orientation to India's education system refer to several questions and problems that arose in the wake of Gandhi's idea of using handicrafts as the organising principle of the curriculum. Some of the questions might seem to have a merely historical value today, but they are nevertheless worth recording. The most controversial question was whether the introduction of handicrafts can make the school an economically productive institution.

Gandhi had, in fact, suggested that productive activity that is centred in traditional handicrafts could enable the school to sustain itself financially. A lot of hostility that basic education programmes had to face undoubtedly arose from this idea, its opponents arguing that productive schools would become factories of child labour. Historically, it would appear, that Gandhi's emphasis on making schools self-sustaining was related to his understandable repugnance towards the use of revenue earned from the sale of liquor for children's education.

As time went by and experience showed both the practical difficulties and limitations of using children's manual work to generate financial resources, the idea took the form of contributions towards school upkeep. Apparently, even this was not acceptable to many, as we can deduce from an official publication written by G. Ramachandran, an eminent exponent of basic education. In a monograph published by the Government of India in 1957, he wrote that 'the main object of productive work is education through such work and income is only a corollary.' He also took pains to clarify that the productive work given to children 'should be such that children can do it without any undue physical strain... Sweated child labour is the very negation of basic education and will defeat it completely.'[2]

This controversy over productive manual work need not divert our attention today from an aspect of Gandhi's educational proposal which can be said to constitute its core. This was the idea of work as participative action. Gandhi believed in work as a means whereby human beings can realise not only their material requirements, but also their intellectual, emotional, and spiritual needs. It is under conditions of social injustice and oppression that work becomes drudgery and a crude weapon directed against all that makes people human. Basic education defined work in its broadest sense so as to make it a medium of socialising the child into a participative culture. Individual autonomy and consent to participate in group responsibility were essential to this socialising agenda.

In this emphasis on participative action, basic education was consistent with modern pedagogical theory which suggests that children's accomplishment in learning new skills and knowledge depends on their consent to learn, to value the teacher's effort, and to work in groups. Two eminent contemporaries of Gandhi, Tagore and Gijubhai, devoted themselves to building institutional models where teaching with the child's consent and participation would be the norm.

Our present system of education fails so often to achieve its aims because the institutional atmosphere, the curriculum, class size, and the methods of teaching ignore the role of the child in education. An erroneous belief commonly reflected in statements of intent is that teachers must *make* the child active. Such statements reveal our neglect, or rather ignorance, of the child's nature which is to be active. All that schools need to do is to ensure that the child's natural desire to be active is not curbed; rather, that this desire is given the opportunity and the means of enhancement through convivial action.

The idea that schools should provide children with the opportunity and the means to undertake skilled manual work was obviously to establish in the minds of children the dignity of work, and not just the intellectual work traditionally provided by schools. But manual work, especially in the context of routine tasks related to school upkeep, was also designed to inculcate initiative, in place of indifference and reluctance to take personal responsibility. Gandhi's life, and not just his educational proposal, shows that his ultimate mission was to awaken in a colonised people the courage to have faith in choice and initiative. Once he had succeeded in arousing this faith in the context of colonial rule, Gandhi extended the scope of choice to include in it a change in the culturally defined antipathy towards manual work, especially when it meant cleaning.

Gandhi's message is a refusal to cope with the given situation. It forms the first step towards taking personal responsibility for one's work. Translated in terms of pedagogical theory, it would mean habituating children to feel responsible out of a personal urge rather than out of the need to comply with someone's orders. Institutional ethos is the primary means of creating such a habit, but the curriculum must highlight this goal as a formal objective ranking higher than literacy or numeracy.

Giving Gandhi's 'new education' a second hearing today would require that we look at autonomy and initiative from the teacher's perspective as well. It can hardly be expected that teachers who are themselves not used to exercising autonomy can encourage children to be autonomous. The ability to take independent decisions and the desire to take personal responsibility must figure as major objectives of teacher training. This, though, cannot be sufficient to ensure that training in such objectives will be actually put into practice. The physical conditions under which elementary teachers work, the rule structures that govern their career and the culture of the offices where teachers are obliged to be a part in order to fulfil administrative routines—all of these constitute an important part of the legacy of colonial rule against which Gandhi had struggled.

The official routines and rules that govern the lives and careers of teachers to this day almost prohibit independent thinking and ingenuity. Even in purely academic matters as shaping the curriculum and selecting pedagogical material, obsolete procedures and expectations continue to hold sway even as new ideas are advocated as being more preferable. Young teachers often get a shock when they discover that an initiative taken by them was not welcomed. During the fifties when basic education was widely practised, inspectorial norms and procedures were found to be at fault and presented problems for pedagogical change. Teachers who attempted to switch from textbook-based instruction to organising activities were often criticised for being over-enthusiastic. Even today, inspectorial expectations are tied to the old, syllabus-covering approach. More than teachers, it is often the monitoring officials who fail to realise that the two kinds of approaches are entirely different and cannot be evaluated on similar criteria.

While we prepare ourselves to rediscover Gandhi's legacy and define it for our times, we can greatly benefit by drawing a few lessons from past experience of basic education. The abandoning of basic education in the early sixties in many parts of the country for its alleged failure need not be regarded as a permanent stigma. The destiny of educational ideas, as indeed of all ideas, is shaped by historical circumstances. It would be foolish to disqualify an idea for fresh trial just because the shape it took at a certain point in history proved unsatisfactory. In any case, the opinion that basic education failed in the first round is questionable. Many basic education institutions carried out excellent programmes in the heyday of Gandhi's ideas, and some continue their battle against all possible odds to this day. In Gujarat, basic education is still a part of the official policy, and at Siksha Niketan in the Burdwan district of West Bengal, a basic school was started as recently as 1987 in memory of Acharya Pramathanath Mukhopadhyay. In the context of teacher training, the programmes offered at Gandhi Vidyapith at Vedchchi and Lok Bharati at Sanosara mark a considerable departure from the usual training available elsewhere in the country.

It is apparently as a 'national' system that basic education failed to live up to the expectations created by it in the forties and fifties. Such a feeling should inspire us to examine the nature of the expectations and the nature of the efforts that were made to fulfil them. The prime expectation was that basic education would bring about social transformation. For this kind of vast rather amorphous hope to be fulfilled, one key condition would have to be a *supportive socio-economic and political climate.* A sustained trial for a long period is another major condition. All evidence points to the fact that basic education had to face a hostile socio-economic climate, and that the quality of political support it received varied from region to region. Indeed, the main reason why basic education could not be sustained for more than a decade or so after Independence was the ambivalence of political patronage.

Political patronage apart, even popular appreciation of basic education was far from adequate. A rather limited attempt was made to create popular interest in the idea, especially to counter common misunderstandings about it which many parents evidently entertained. Perhaps it was assumed that the idea was simple, so it would be easily understood and appreciated. It also appears that concerted opposition to it was never expected. Some of those who supported basic education as a policy tried to defend it when it was attacked, others responded merely by staying quietly committed to their daily work. It is hard to find a case where the critics of basic education were asked to give an alternative to the traditional system of children's education.

For a revival of Gandhi's concept of education as a guide to general reform today, the lesson is obvious: attention must be given to the creation of a receptive socio-political climate. A second lesson we might learn from the past concerns the flexibility and diversity of approaches. Looking back at the fifties, one finds that an orthodox interpretation of Gandhi's proposal was prevalent. It was reflected in the uniformity of curricular choices, training procedures, and administrative arrangements. This was obviously a major contradiction, considering that Gandhi was among the strongest critics of the uniformity that colonial rule had imposed on schools in India. In this matter, basic education became a victim of the bureaucratic culture entrenched in the education system.

In a revived basic education programme, local and regional *diversity of approaches* must be encouraged as a matter of principle and not just tolerated. But diversity cannot be triggered by pressing a button, especially when it has been discouraged for so long and when the bias against it is so deep rooted in policy and planning. Indeed, the capacity to evolve a local style has atrophied among teachers owing to long disuse. And the capacity we are talking about is not an outcome of training alone; it also depends on mental attributes such as the desire to experiment, and culturally transmitted attributes such as self-reliance and acceptance of risk. A diversity of approaches will have to be encouraged in a sustained manner for it to become a part of the system. One step towards such encouragement would be to create a climate featuring an appreciation of diversity.

The works of three eminent Indian philosophers are of great help in creating a positive social ethos for a policy which might guarantee teachers' freedom to organise the daily curriculum differently round common themes. These philosophers are Sri Aurobindo, Rabindranath Tagore, and J. Krishnamurti. Their writings on education, not easily accessible today, need to be widely disseminated as part of the initiative to promote a variety of approaches in a revised basic education programme.

The lack of diversity was reflected most sharply in the choice of agriculture and gardening as 'crafts' to be taught at school. This choice was apparently based on the requirement we have discussed earlier, namely that basic schools should strive towards financial self-sufficiency. The fact that agricultural activity or gardening would generate usable produce and possibly cash, perhaps clouded the recognition that this kind of manual activity could hardly be called a handicraft.

The training for precision and accuracy required by traditional handicrafts cannot be associated with the manual work involved in agriculture and gardening. In fact, the excessive emphasis given to agricultural production at some basic education institutions led to complaints that children were being used as labourers, lending further weight to the already prevalent prejudice against basic schools. The joy of learning a handicraft and the refinement of the senses that it can be expected to bring about in childhood, cannot be conveniently associated with production-oriented agricultural work.

A crippling blow was suffered by the post-Independence programme of basic education when the schools practising it were denied recognition for higher studies and examinations in certain parts of the country. This structural discord significantly curtailed the options available to children studying in basic schools. The denial of recognition of their work was based on the argument that they had not followed the syllabus and textbooks prescribed in the other schools. The attempt made in basic schools to displace the prescribed textbook from its dominant position in Indian school life proved the single most problematic aspect of basic education, as far as its image in state offices of education was concerned. Teachers in basic schools were trained to develop their own daily curriculum of activities and their own material. They were supposed to avoid using the textbook in the early grades, and keep it to the minimum in later grades. In this practice they were following Gandhi's articulate distaste for textbook-centred instruction, which was clearly a part of his general rejection of colonial education. Gandhi had written,

> If textbooks are treated as a vehicle for education, the living world of the teacher has very little value. A teacher who teaches from textbooks does not impart originality to his pupils. He himself becomes a slave of textbooks and has no opportunity or occasion to be original. It therefore seems that the less textbooks there are the better it is for the teacher and his pupils.[4]

But teaching without textbooks made the inspectorial bureaucracy feel uncomfortable, and that was one reason why basic schools had so much trouble to gain accreditation on par with other schools.

Even today, when voluntary agencies engaged in innovative work attempt to replace the prescribed textbook with other material, they have to face the difficult task of convincing the bureaucracy that the work they are doing is as serious as the work normal schools are doing with textbooks. Apparently, the colonial practice of prescribing textbooks continues to fulfil some deep psychological function in the system of education and in the society it serves. Even parents get apprehensive about the quality of instruction when it is not squarely based on the prescribed text. Understandably, parents who belong to an economically weaker strata of society get particularly suspicious about such instruction because school textbooks are the only books in their houses. The textbook symbolises authentic and approved knowledge, the ultimate proof of its indispensability being that the examination is based on it. The prescribed textbook, thus, forms the hub of a structure of relationships governing the system of education.

The past experience of basic education provides us with an excellent guide to train and motivate the teacher to plan his or her own daily curriculum and assemble appropriate material to execute the plan. The same past experience warns us that such laudable changes in teaching might create misconceptions among parents and officers if textbooks are denigrated or dispensed with. We need to look at the textbook itself in our search for a solution to this problem. There is no theoretical reason why textbooks should demean the teacher's work, as Gandhi had found they were doing, or the child's natural urge to be active. If textbooks have such tragic consequences, the fault might lie to a great extent with the textbooks themselves and with the syllabus which they supposedly follow.

The report of the Yashpal committee, which was appointed by the Government of India in the early 1990s to examine the widespread problem of curricular burden on children, found Indian textbooks to be greatly deficient in terms of the capacity to arouse children's interest and involvement in learning.[5] As this report suggests, our textbooks seldom require children to observe the world round them or to engage in purposive activity. Some textbooks do list classroom activities in a routine manner. Often, these activities are of the kind that cannot be organised in an ordinary classroom. And what children might learn from these activities is stated anyhow.

On the score of arousing interest, modern textbooks often fare worse than the textbooks written in Gandhi's day. But all such deficiencies can be overcome if textbooks are written with greater care and with the active participation of teachers. The training given to teachers in the old programme of basic education to prepare classroom material can be incorporated in the future as an enhanced, more general preparation for participation in textbook writing.

A fresh initiative using Gandhi's educational thought must break new ground in conceptualising relevant knowledge for today's children. It should also be an improvement on the past experience of basic education in areas where it revealed structural and practical problems. The psychological insights into childhood that are available to us now should also be reflected in the new programme. The following core areas might form an attractive curricular design for a revived basic education programme:

Core area I	Core area II	Core area III	Core area IV
Health and hygiene Nature study Social study	Heritage craft (e.g. weaving). Toycraft, clay work or any other handicraft	Expressive arts Reading Writing	Mathematics Sorting and representation of quantitative information

The four core areas named above can be expected to provide opportunities to extend children's experiential base and knowledge as they advance from grade one to five. These core areas can also supply a basis for further classification of knowledge in the remaining grades of elementary education, namely grades six to eight.

Two aspects of this curricular design that deserve some elaboration are nature study and heritage crafts. In the present elementary-level science curriculum, nature study has the latent purpose of imparting a sense of conquest or control over nature. Such an idea is quite contrary to Gandhi's vision of a world where human beings and nature might coexist. It also clashes with the widely accepted current knowledge of ecological balance and sustainability, for example, in the context of disease control with the help of poisons. The contradictions involved in such strategies are noticed by children long before they are acknowledged, and that too reluctantly, in the school. The confusion and cynicism that this delayed acknowledgement causes can be avoided if school pedagogy provides for nature study in the context of a holistic vision of life and health.

The inclusion of heritage crafts in the elementary school curriculum can be expected to make a unique contribution which would combine several different educational aims. These would include the imparting of manual skill and dexterity, aesthetic sense, and the development of certain aspects of personality which the traditional school curriculum and culture routinely fail to develop. These aspects relate to self-esteem arising from a sense of worth and confidence in one's competence. The teaching of heritage crafts in childhood can stem the large-scale de-skilling of young people that is taking place as a result of poorly conceived modernisation. In association with the expressive arts (such as music, drawing and painting), handicrafts can provide that much needed training of the senses on which alone the development of meaningful literacy skills can take place.

Specific activities and topics of study that would fill up these core areas ought to be identified at regional and local levels. For this exercise, the following ideas can perhaps be treated as guiding principles derived from Gandhi's legacy and child psychology:

- The child's immediate milieu is treated as a resource for itemising required knowledge and skills (for example, local birds, flowers, crops and trees; local language and folklore; and locally practised crafts and expressive arts);
- all topics are taught with the help of activities. These activities may be the ones suggested in a curriculum guideline or they may be new ones, devised by the teacher;
- children are trained to work in small groups;
- classroom activities aim to extend to the child's life at home;
- some activities provide opportunities which require children to work outside the classroom every day;
- a few topics are selected for deeper probing which might take several days, taking the shape of a project; and
- children are given opportunities to work independently of the teacher.

The acceptance of these guiding principles will demand a major initiative towards changing present-day teacher training. In planning such an initiative, we can realistically hope to find useful ideas in the literature that document the basic education programmes of the fifties and in the ongoing training programmes of certain Gandhian institutions.

One organisational change which might greatly assist in realising a key goal of basic education would be to amalgamate community-level health services with the local elementary school. It is a common experience that village-level health workers have closer ties with the community than the school teacher. The situation does, of course, vary according to region, but in general the health worker seems to have a more personal acquaintance with parents and children than the teacher has. The health worker is also usually better equipped than the teacher to look after children's health-related problems and to advise them on such problems. Incorporating the health worker's services with the school will enhance the school's capacity to work for children's welfare. The isolated and meagre instruction which the school provides at present seldom succeeds in making health and hygiene prime concerns of practical knowledge for the growing child.

A similar step needs to be taken in the context of the services currently provided under Integrated Child Development Services (ICDS) programmes for early childhood care and pre-school education. It is ironical that the services made available under this programme in thousands of villages remain isolated from school, even though the services are aimed at making children's transition to school smoother. Separating these services from the school has exacerbated the confusion in the community's mind over the nature and function of different institutions. Such confusion hardly helps in motivating the community to participate in the running of these institutions. A truly integrated set of child-related programmes will surely have a better chance of inspiring people to take active interest in these programmes and to feel responsible towards them. Such integration will be compatible with the holistic vision of community welfare embedded in the idea of basic education.

Finally, a new programme of basic education must address the task of creating conditions in which the teacher can establish contact with the community and the family. Planners of basic education in the fifties had, for this purpose, chalked out school designs that would include housing for teachers.[6] We need to revisit the plans for housing made at that time, for the problem it attempted to deal with still afflicts the system of elementary education. In fact, it has become more acute. The daily commuting by hundreds of thousands of elementary school teachers to their village school and back on public transport represents a tragic waste of their energy and modest personal resources. It also represents a major loss for the children and the community which the teacher is supposed to serve.

By enabling teachers to become a part of the spatial community we can hope to enhance their involvement in children's out-of-school life. The goal of a Gandhian plan of educational reconstruction can be only to make teachers responsible for the overall development of the children they work with. Progress in this direction will depend on the extent to which bureaucratic control over schools and teachers is replaced by a system of accountability, jointly managed by teachers and the community. The degradation suffered by elementary-level teachers at the hands of officials is the single most relevant reason why teachers greet every reform with cynicism and resignation. This attitude cannot be countered without making alterations in entrenched styles of financial and administrative control. Decision-making and power are involved in each micro-detail of routine functioning of the system. These micro-details can be visualised as so many screws of a giant colonial machine. The best of ideas aimed at winning the teacher's heart and the community's support get crushed under these screws. A new programme of basic education can hardly be expected to work if these screws remain intact.

In the context of emerging policies, a programme of basic education inspired by Gandhi's social ideals will undoubtedly face formidable ideological challenges, and also organisational ones. What is being called 'globalisation' is, by all indications that we have at present, a process whereby neo-colonial arrangements of domination are seeking legitimacy. These arrangements have the potential to threaten just about every social and economic ideal we associate with Gandhi. Traditional communities are facing a direct assault from the forces of commercialisation. In a context where many communities are facing extreme forms of deprivation, their formal empowerment under the banner of grass-root democracy promises little relief. In urban centres too, mass disemployment seems to be the norm triggered by the drive to embrace microchip-based technologies in an indiscriminate manner. The genetic modification of foodcrops also suggests a course along which multinational corporations, and the wealthy nations where these corporations are based, will consolidate their hold on Indian agriculture. In this larger scenario, Gandhi's ideas will have to be used as a channel of pervasive resistance if a programme of basic education is to have a substantial chance of success, even on a small scale —as a niche within the system or outside it. More than truth and non-violence, then, Gandhi must symbolise 'the gift of the fight' in which Marjorie Sykes found the kernel of his teachings.[7]

Notes

1. The written version of this speech appeared in *Democracy and Education in India*, edited by Krishna Kumar and published by Radiant, Delhi (1993) under the auspices of the Nehru Memorial Museum and Library, New Delhi.
2. John Dewey, *The Public and Its Problems* (New York: Henry Holt, 1927; reprint, Athens: Swallow Press, Ohio University, 1991).
3. G. Ramachandran, *Orienting Primary Schools Towards the Basic Pattern* (Ministry of Education, Government of India, New Delhi, 1957): 4.
4. M.K. Gandhi, 'Text Books', *Harijan*, 9 December 1939.
5. *Learning Without Burden* (Ministry of Human Resource Development, Government of India. New Delhi, 1993).
6. *Report on Primary-Junior Basic Schools* (National Buildings Organisation. Ministry of Works and Housing, New Delhi, undated).
7. Marjorie Sykes and Jahangir Patel, *Gandhi: The Gift of the Fight* (Rasulia, Hoshangabad: Friends' Rural Centre, 1995).

10

The Concept of Quality in Education

Using the term 'quality' in the context of education evokes a natural reluctance, yet the temptation to distinguish two institutions, even systems, in terms of the quality of what they offer, is equally strong. Neither the reluctance nor the temptation is particularly difficult to explain. The reluctance one feels when speaking of quality in education has to do with the fear that we might trivialise the concept of education or injure its core if we subject it to the kinds of checks that are applied to judge quality in material objects like cars or in experiences like travel. We hesitate to let education be judged by so-called quality standards because we associate education per se with a certain quality or character. Can education devoid of quality be called education at all, we rightly ask, and by asking such a question, realise that there is a characteristic experience involved in an educative process which is essential and therefore non-negotiable. It is only when we might be forced to describe this characteristic aspect of an educational experience that we notice the first stirrings of the temptation to use the word 'quality' to distinguish minimum from maximum or intermediary levels in characterising the experience of education offered by an institution or system. We feel tempted to say that the quality of institution 'A' or a course it offers is better than institution 'B' because one or more characteristic features of education is relatively stronger at institution 'A'.

Recent Context

This brief introductory analysis reminds us of the two meanings of the term 'quality', both of which are relevant to the recent history of the quality debate.[1] The first meaning refers to the essential attribute with which something may be identified, and the second meaning refers to the rank or superiority of one thing over another. The quality debate persists at least partly because sufficient attention is not paid to the tension that arises between the two meanings when the term 'quality' is applied to education. In the recent past, quality as a concern has dominated the educational debates triggered and sustained by international aid and cooperation, and by the ethos of economic globalisation. Most, if not all, of these debates have been steeped in a neo-liberal perspective on the political economy. This perspective and the approach to education which is associated with it, have found reflection in national systems of education in many countries of the colonised world, India being no exception to this trend. Even in the case of the wealthier countries of the so-called developed world, educational research and writing of recent years has reflected the dominance of the neo-liberal perspective (which will be discussed below).

In the 'developing' world, the popularity of the cross-country frame of reference which any discussion of quality necessarily invokes, has to do with the progress made towards universalisation of access to primary education, particularly since the Jomtien conference of 1979.[2] The dimension of haste, which is rather too apparent in discussions of globalisation, and inevitably hints at the dire implications of delayed response to the remedies suggested by institutions like the International Monetary Fund, has influenced the contemporary discourse of quality in education. Setting dates for developing countries to reach certain goals is a part of this phenomenon. The currently popular perception that the time to focus on quality issues has arrived because access goals have been more or less achieved as far as the primary part of the elementary level of education is concerned, is a part of this discourse. In the case of India, the dichotomisation of access and quality actively guided policy choices like the appointment of para-teachers and programmes like the Education Guarantee Scheme (EGS) and the District Primary Education Programme (DPEP) during the 1990s. The impact of these schemes highlights how long-term damage can be instituted in a system by way of pursuing short-term goals, notwithstanding criticisms even at the time of implementation. The systemic liability that initiatives of this kind have imposed on governments is now becoming clear in many states, with Madhya Pradesh serving as a piquant example of how extreme compliance with the remedies for expansion suggested by global advisors during the 1990s, has resulted in the widespread degradation of its education system.

Over the last two decades, the imperative to monitor the growth of access and quality within each country and across countries, has gained acceptance in a global institutional environment marked by interest in the geographical expansion of markets of both goods and labour. Support for an export-oriented economy and acceptance of multinational corporations as partners in development are among the indicators of the new policy environment relevant to education. This environment has unfolded in diverse ways. In India, the policy focus on universalisation has conveyed the message that education cannot be regarded as a privilege as it once was. This message provides support for the argument that universal access must mean education of comparable quality for all children.[3] In the global context, such a plea for quality—along with universal access—has acted as a moral stick for 'developmentalism', which can be described as an ideology to promote the life-style of the developed West by the selective use of its norms as indicators of a universally accessible 'good' life. But the real power and contemporary relevance of the argument for quality come from the need to regulate the flow of dependable labour, expertise and knowledge in the globalised economy. Although it is a matter of debate whether the so-called 'knowledge economy' is a reality or merely an ideology, the extent to which its discussion routinely clubs the growth of Information and Communication Technology (ICT) with the growth of quality in education implies considerable diminution or trivialisation of the concept of education. When ICT is mention as a means to add value to, and thereby inject quality, into access, education is reduced to the transfer of information.

Far from showing concern for any essential attributes of education, much of the current usage of the term 'quality' focuses on the relatively more instrumentalist features of education. Whereas one might expect 'quality' to refer to a comprehensive or holistic view of education, contemporary debates on quality often stick to the limited view of learning which became synonymous with behaviouristic educational theory and pedagogy. According to this theory and the pedagogic advice it offers, learning is something that can be planned, predicted and accurately measured once it has occurred.[4] Quality-related writing and research around the world, and not just in developing countries, has attached great significance to large-scale testing. Of course, not all testing is behaviouristic in its orientation, but mass testing does tend to encourage teaching for predictable outcomes. Outcome-orientation has also gained popularity in the context of financial accountability. Thus, 'outcome' or 'result', 'transparency' and 'accountability' have become essential parts of the discourse of quality in education. Emphasis placed on these dimensions of the execution of policy has diminished the acknowledgement of intrinsic motivation, diversity of styles and context-specificity as values in both teaching and learning. The predominance of quality as a global concern today cannot be delinked from this historical regression, and not just stagnation, in the concept of learning as reflected in policy or systemic discourses.

Quality and Equality

We can now appreciate an element of irony in the current quality debate. On the one hand, the concern for quality in education is an expression of the moral imperative of equality and justice, inasmuch as education is no more regarded a privilege; while on the other hand, it assists the management of universalisation by facilitating the separation of access from substance. On account of this irony, the quality debate has failed to retain the idea of quality as a characteristic of education, as opposed to something that adds value to it. One consequence of this failure is that a minimalist programme of education appears to constitute a valid step towards universalisation. In many countries, including India, the programme is so minimalist that it offers little more than access to a building called the school. Under the haste-oriented ethos of globalisation, this kind of minimalism invites the creation of islands of excellence where the nation's so-called competitive edge can be sharpened while the larger system prepares for transition from mere access to infusion of an ingredient called quality. This argument proposes a basic tension or contradiction between equality and quality, suggesting that as a systemic goal equality can only nurture quantity, while quality would require regulation of equality.

The ideology of neo-liberalism, which constitutes an essential background to the recent usage of 'quality' in the context of education, emphasises 'choice' and its enhancement as a goal of economic and educational reform or restructuring. Supporters of state-withdrawal and increased room for private initiative in education have mooted and pushed several new proposals structured around the idea of 'choice' in the recent past, and in each case the plea has been justified in the name of 'quality'. Private universities, fast-track teacher education programmes, NGO-run in-service training, and vouchers are among the many topics on which neo-liberal advocacy has referred to quality as a concern which can be addressed by increasing consumer choice in types and modes and the providers of educational services. In order to understand and deal with this approach, we need to examine how quality and choice seem interlinked, and then how choice appears to become synonymous with *agency*, a term which has also gained popularity in education in the recent decades. Its current popularity can be cited to two resource orbits from which its present-day meaning draws substance: one, the cognitive revolution which insisted that children have agency which makes them inborn learners; and two, the various activist movements which aimed at imparting agency to the marginalised. In both orbits, the meaning came from the idea that someone who had agency exercised freedom. The relevant question to ask is whether this was the *freedom to make choices*? This is an important question, because neo-liberalism, as an ideology, benefits a great deal from the vague similarity we can find between choice and agency. As a term, 'choice' is deeply rooted in the history of liberalism of which contemporary neo-liberalism is an extremist, necessarily primitivised version. The main distinction between the two terms is that 'agency' has an inventive connotation which 'choice' does not, because choice is between things already invented. Inasmuch as education is related to the human capacity for setting new goals for oneself and the world, and not merely to pursue given goals, we can regard the capacity of imparting agency as an intrinsic characteristic, and hence an indicator of quality of education. The capacity to provide and improve choice is a very limited goal for education, because it treats the universe as a given.

In the Indian context, the seeming dichotomy between quality and equality is best encapsulated by a metaphor used by a major architect of India's education policy after independence, namely the late J.P. Naik.[5] The sub-title of his book describes quality, equality and quantity as an 'elusive triangle' constituting a policy dilemma. Revisiting the concept of quality as a characteristic and therefore inseparable feature of education helps us recognise why the triangle is actually illusory, implying that its elusiveness has been historically constructed by poor conceptualisation of policy choices. Since comparison is an important meaning of quality, the chances of any national system's capacity to compete with others can be construed as being dependent on its ability to identify its own best products in a fair and open manner. If competition is the best way to identity talent, it follows that talent selected from the widest possible pool of human diversity, in all its forms, will have greater predictable quality than the talent selected from a narrower pool. Moreover, from this point of view, if talent is drawn from a narrow pool, the drawing process will become reproductive, making the competitive quality of the talent drawn weaker with every successive round of selection. Hence, in this line of thought, it would be correct to conclude that equality is an aspect of quality, not contradictory to it. On the basis of this conclusion we can say that national systems which are fair and open to all entrants will compete better in a globalised set-up because the children selected through such systems for successive stages of retention and longer experience of education, will have the best skills needed for competitive survival.

Although this view helps us remove the seeming gap or opposition between quality and equality, it distracts us from the first meaning of quality in education, namely its intrinsic character and the logic of its force. The point about quality and equality being linked inadvertently takes on a social-Darwinist character, through its support to the view that competition necessarily brings out quality by giving the best a chance to be recognised. Such a view has a commonsensical value in the context of education. It is often argued, and quite persuasively too, that students differ in terms of their brilliance, and that we must distinguish the brilliant from the less brilliant if we want to use education efficiently as a means of nation-building or in order to make a nation globally competitive. Such a view gains further strength in its persuasive capacity when its advocates say that brilliance must be recognised and encouraged irrespective of gender, class, caste or region. Attractive as this position is, it misses the role and capacity education has for enabling the less competitive, and in that sense 'less brilliant' of today, to acquire characteristics that might make them more competitive in the course of time.

This capacity of education arises out of its nature, in the sense that education works in rather long time-horizons, both in the lives of individuals, and more so, in the life of collectivities defined by caste, class or gender. If certain aspects of the life in these groupings induce a lack of educational merit or brilliance today, there is every reason to believe (i.e. if one believes in the instrumentality of education as supporters of competitive equality do) that the brilliance-reducing function of such groupings will weaken or diminish over time. Individuals belonging to them will then be able to compete more equally with other individuals, satisfying the supporters of a competitive approach to quality as a prime concern in education today.

This possibility may be averted if education is conceptualised and planned within narrow time-horizons or to address only present-day challenges. Globalisation presents precisely this kind of scenario, not directly through its nature, but rather as a harbinger of fiscal austerity vis-à-vis social services, particularly health and education, for governments in developing countries such as India. The accompanying discourse and its translation into real terms, namely financial constraints for education funding, circumvents the notion that education is a long-term capital investment, that is, in human capital, whose current-day value cannot be accurately measured only in present expenditure, but must include future payoffs as well. Without this acknowledgement of long-term gains, education expenditures can appear worthy only of minimisation. On the other hand, the satirical view would be that acknowledging the long-term benefits from education would deprive economists and managers of the popular challenge of making education more 'efficient' in providing a 'bang for the buck'. The consequent loss of importance for education would have to be balanced against the parallel risk of education losing its identity that we run by continuing with the current, short-horizon conceptualisation.

Wider Perspective

The apparent dichotomy between quality and equality needs to be seen from a larger perspective. The phrase 'quality of life' provides such a perspective by pushing the two meanings of quality to come closer. When we speak of quality in the context of so encompassing a category as life itself, it becomes difficult to distinguish the first meaning of quality as a core characteristic of an object or experience from its second meaning, that of a means of comparison. This is so because life is an all-inclusive idea. Any attempt to compare life in its totality in two situations or contexts would necessarily draw attention to the disparities of life experiences. Less disparity would mean greater overall quality. This is precisely the argument put forward by Wilkinson and Pickett[6] in their study of economic growth in relation to its social outcomes. They find that positive social outcomes as indicators of the quality of life, are found more copiously in societies with greater equality, than in others which are economically rich but more unequal. Though the focus of this study is health, its perspective is relevant to education. Both health and education nurture enabling conditions for human life except for the fact that advantages of education are arguably more diverse and some of them depend on other enabling conditions. It is hardly possible that good health makes someone unhappy, but someone with education can be unhappy if she cannot find a job but is expected to do so on account of her being educated. In this instance, we may ask whether the capacity to help a person to find a job is a core characteristic of education. As a major modern thinker, Gandhi used this idea to criticise colonial education, but he did so with reference to self-reliance, including the capacity to earn, and not a job as such. This is an important distinction because it draws attention to the twin skill-imparting and disposition-inducing roles of education, which deserve to be perceived as among the core aspects of education, in other words, of its intrinsic quality.

Nuanced Equality

If equality is indeed an aspect of quality, we must ensure that we do not treat equality in a mechanical manner. This is a problem that equality among human beings has always presented to its supporters. Equality can be of various types, depending upon the context; therefore, we need to contemplate what kind of equality is most relevant to education. Given the fact that education is not a one-time experience but rather something which tends to grow and change with the growth of the learner, it is necessary to look at equality in the context of each individual's own unique way of growing. Universality cannot mean uniformity, even to a limited degree, if equality is to be treated as an aspect of quality in a characteristically educational way. Demands of managing a vast system normally imply that control passes upwards, from learners and teachers to those placed in more central authoritative positions. In a state-run system, such authorities are bureaucratic; in a privately run system, authority passes into the hands of managers and financial providers. If an educational system or institution succumbs to the pressures and the natural-looking demands of such authorities, it will compromise with quality in education even if the product has the gloss and finish of a well-designed car or hygienically packed cornflakes. Private schools which advertise their air-conditioned classrooms and close-circuit television cameras refer to their quality in precisely this confused sense. Educational quality requires that the learner retains some control in his or her own growth and the teacher remains autonomous enough to respond to the learner rather than to orders from above, or demands that emanate from parents or the market.

A parallel case needs to be made for defining quality in a manner relevant to each of the categories that currently demarcate inequality—gender, caste, a tribal or peasant background and the like. Such differentiated or nuanced treatment is necessary because quality, as an experiential aspect of education, is likely to pose a specific challenge for children belonging to the diverse social categories which, under the present system, suffer from inequality. Specific forms of implicit discrimination characterise the quality of education—or rather the lack of it—in a classroom unaware or insensitive to inequality. In the case of a tribal child this can mean language-inequality, while for a child from a scheduled caste this can mean discrimination at the hands of fellow pupils and the teacher. To describe this phenomenon in some detail, and illustrate how a school must knowledgably structure educational quality, given a background of inequality, the case of gender is explored as an example.

There can be little doubt about the proposition that the experience of education for girls in general remains poor in its quality, because the conditions under which they acquire this experience are rife with reminders of their inequality (to boys). Discrimination in pedagogic settings in the classroom, as well as in other spheres of school life, does not allow girls to fulfil their intellectual potential. Supposing that a school did accomplish success in overcoming or disallowing discrimination against girls in all spheres of activity, this would enhance the quality of girls' educational experience, but not in all its aspects. In certain aspects its quality would remain thin or poor if the school made no attempt to compensate for the inequality girls suffer in the world outside the school, at home and elsewhere, in experiences unrelated to life at school. Social anthropologist Leela Dube[7] has analytically documented the socialising experiences girls are subjected to from infancy onwards. Restrictions on their natural child-like agility, inculcation of the anxiety-causing awareness that leaving one's natal home is an inescapable aspect of womanhood, and the mental fixing of matrimony and motherhood as the sole purposes of life are among the common aspects of cultural imprinting girls are subjected to. With the arrival of puberty, the imprinting regime gets harsher. A culturally sanctioned ideology of impurity is assiduously cultivated in relation to the female body. Negative dispositions of this kind and the values they are linked to, such as acceptance of subjugation and the inferiority, are totally incompatible with the aims of education. If the school does not address this kind of negative mental baggage girls come with, it can hardly be seen as providing an education which claims quality because it equips them to compete with boys merely in a mechanically equal sense.

For education to provide gender equality, and thereby claim quality, its experience would have to include specific curricular and pedagogic devices which address the deeper sources of gender inequality, including the sources located outside the school, at home and in the cultural universe. This compensatory aspect of equality is important inasmuch as it offsets or reverses the restraining or curbing influences of inequality on a child's capacity for learning at school. The moot point is that quality of education at school cannot be viewed in isolation from the larger universe in which a child's growth unfolds, simply because the school's attempt to improve the quality of its education-provision depends for its success on the child's freedom to benefit from the school's attempt. Freedom signifies a condition where restraining influences have been removed. To what extent freedom can be enhanced by education alone, without the cooperation of larger social, and especially cultural forces, is a different question.

Notes

1. K. Kumar and P. Sarangapani, 'History of the Quality Debate', *Contemporary Education Dialogue*, 2: 1 (Monsoon 2004) 30–52.
2. K. Kumar, M. Priyam and S. Saxena, 'Looking Beyond the Smokescreen: DPEP and Primary Education in India', *Economic and Political Weekly*, 36: 7 (17 February 2001) 560–68.
3. UNESCO, *Education for All: The Quality Imperative* (Global Monitoring Report) (Paris: UNESCO, 2005).
4. Lawrenece Stenhouse, *An Introduction to Curriculum Research and Development* (London: Heinemann, 1975).
5. J.P. Naik, *Equality, Quality and Quantity: The Elusive Triangle of Indian Education* (New Delhi: Allied Publishers, 1975).
6. R. Wilkinson and K. Pickett, *The Spirit Level: Why More Equal Societies Almost Always Do Better* (London: Allen Lane, 2009).
7. Leela Dubey, *Anthropological Explorations in Gender* (New Delhi: Sage, 2007).

11

Technology and Education Today

Education and technology have a common tendency to offer transformative visions of the world. These visions are often romantic and utopian. Policy documents in education present a predictable future which can be shaped and planned according to priorities and needs. On the other hand, the romantic vision of transformation offered by technology focuses on making the world more efficient and convenient. Its efficiency is related to computers, their speed and capacity to process vast amounts of information. We are already in a time where it is believed that technology can offer us solutions to just about anything, including problems that arise from unethical behaviour. CCTVs will assist not only the police to find out if anyone has misused the airport, for stealing, for example, they will also be useful to a school principal to find out if the teacher has taught the lesson according to prescribed norms. The combined visions of education and technology are quite popular today. Education is believed to offer us ways that might bring the technological

---

Krishna Kumar, 'Technology and Education Today', Social Change 52(4). pp. 467–477, 2022. Copyright (c) CSD 2022. DOI: 10.1177/00490857221134925

vision of transformation closer. So all that education is expected to do is teach the young how to use the new information and communication technology for reaping all its benefits, including those that we can already see and others that are latent. Education, in that sense, is expected to serve the goal of the transformation of the world that technology promises, for improving the efficiency with which the world runs today. Education has been assigned a subservient role in the service of the world that technology will create and manage.

Let us examine these transformative visions by looking closely at their 'real' worlds, meaning the everyday life they inhabit in practice. The real world of education is messy. Its messiness can be explained by noticing that education is a relational activity. It involves all the unpredictable elements of a human relationship. A teacher engages with a student—somebody who is quite different, different in the sense of age, and therefore in the sense of the historical moment in which he or she acquired this consciousness of being a student or a certain desire to pursue knowledge. When a teacher relates to someone born much later than himself or herself, the teacher becomes, through this relationship, acutely aware of the limitations of the task and the limited chances of its success. The task involves transfer of knowledge and the possibility that the student will find the knowledge useful, perhaps even inspiring. These are far from predictable, yet policies in education and state discourses of education would make us believe that education can reach predictable goals. No part of the world bears witness to the claim that education can reach its goals. We have plenty of examples, whether of the Soviet Union which has fallen apart, or our own country where we were all supposed to become colonised and not aspire for freedom. Education, had it been successful, would have provided historical continuities of a kind that I do not think historians would have appreciated. When we recognise how unpredictable the outcomes of education are, we get rid of the vision-based, transformative idea of education. In fact what happens is, as the teacher gets older and more experienced, she/he gains humility and the student gains confidence to be independent. The goal of education is reached the day the student achieves freedom from the teacher and does new or unexpected things, and does them independently.

Now let's look briefly at the real world of technology. Going by what Ursula Franklin's analysis reveals, the real world of technology is a social world.[1] If technology as she says is 'how things are done or organised around here' then it is a world which is embedded in social, political and economic conditions. Technologies arise in this real world of social fabric and social relationships, which are also economic relationships, and have their political articulations in various kinds of institutions. Technology is the practice of life under structures that technology offers. It is a world that necessarily practises certain kinds of exclusions in order to achieve the results that it offers. Whenever technology changes, that moment of change is very interesting to watch—because in any moment of technological change, new values arise. No matter whether the change is offered or it is imposed, new patterns of exclusion emerge, because they alone allow the world to be managed. So, every new technology, in the sense of its own real world, attempts to shape the world of social, economic and political relations. If we are attempting to understand the relations of technology with education it is very important for us to keep this real world of technology in mind. Any number of examples would suffice. If technology offers efficiency, convenience and speed, then it is worth asking what kinds of exclusions it designs to take. Consider, for example, online admissions in a university. It certainly offers efficiency and convenience. However, it is important to ask whose convenience and efficiency is achieved by this, whose time is saved, and whose time is actually not saved; what kind of patterns of exclusion arise in a diverse and unequal society. These questions can well be asked. Therefore it is important to study technology particularly in moments of technological change with reference to patterns of exclusion.

In this essay, we will examine the relationship between computer technology and education in three key orbits. These are work, knowledge and ethics. Although the following discussion treats them as separate orbits, they are intertwined in the everyday lives of millions of teachers.

First Orbit: Work

Let us now move towards the three orbits. The first orbit in which we will examine the relations between education and technology is that of work. It is a natural first choice because education has always had very close relations with work. It is widely accepted that education prepares us for the world of work, specifically or generally, depending on what kind of education we have had. Historically, education has spread because it prepares people for work. Today a certain amount of education is expected to become universal, precisely because education seems to have an impact on the capacity of human beings to engage with work. When we look at the word 'work' in the context of education, we can quickly establish a distinction in our mind between work and job. This is an important distinction to hold on to for looking at the relation between education and technology. It appears that the technology that we are talking about is turning all kinds of work into jobs. So if you notice discourses at various levels of politics, industry or economic policy, you will notice that the phrase that has been current for almost a decade now is 'job creation', rather than work creation. Something significant has already happened to dislodge work from its familiar place in our vocabulary: it has been replaced by the word 'job'.

It is important to examine this distinction between the two and notice that these are not synonymous. One thing about work that we could say in a fairly generalisable sense is that what work you do gradually gives you an identity. It does that because as you work, and if you work consistently, then you gradually get better at it, in the sense that a time comes when you begin to say 'Well, this is who I am; I am the person who does that work nicely', or that people know me as 'the person who gets that work done properly'. No matter whether it is work done with your hands, voice or the various tools and technologies: work has that identity-imparting quality or power in it. Whether work is an expression of the human desire to be active and to relate to others through an economic activity are separate issues that will take us too far away from the main theme.

Let us now look at the term 'job'. To begin with, a job is something that is assigned to you. Every job has a beginning and an end; when you finish a job that has been assigned to you, either the person who gave it to you now gives you another job, or else you start looking for another job. But there is no inbuilt assumption or guarantee that the jobs that you get will all be similar, continuous or will require similar capacities from you. In that sense, jobs do not necessarily impart an identity, certainly not a continuous identity. You can say that I am good at doing any job that is assigned to me; and that will be a statement that will show your sense of humour and your ability to cope with difficult times. But it is different from the statement that 'My work so far has allowed me to accumulate a certain capacity or dexterity in doing it'. This is an important distinction to use in the context of the fact that now a lot of work, which barely twenty years ago would have counted as fairly specific and diversified, has been absorbed by computer technology. What this technology has offered us instead is a range of jobs.

In the field of education, the core activity that employs adults is teaching. How computer technology is affecting teaching is a major question for the kind of inquiry we are carrying out. Its primary characteristic is that it is a relational activity in the sense that the daily interaction it involves is indeterminate and its outcomes are often unpredictable. Computer technology offers mediation between the teacher and the student, and thereby shapes what the teacher can or cannot do. In essence, the teacher's job is to regulate the student's encounter with knowledge. The computer is also very good at it and, therefore, it mediates the teacher's relationship with the student in a distinctive sense. But as far as the identity-giving role of work is concerned, we can recognise several problems in the mediating role of the computer. Because teaching is a relational activity, it is necessarily individuating, both for the teacher and the student. It may not always happen, but in its best form teaching is supposed to be individuating. That is what progress in educational thought and practice implies. With the spread of education, more and more children came into the school system, and the difficulty of individuating became increasingly more complex. It is all the more so in societies that have attempted to universalise education.

Individuating poses the same issues across the different stages, that is, primary, secondary and higher education. In the relationship between the teacher and students, recognition of individuality is an important responsibility resting with the former. The computer offers to mediate in the teacher–student relationship through its various devices, such as a scripted curriculum, or a modular lesson or a PowerPoint presentation or any number of ever-increasing conveniences. Replacement of the blackboard with the white, smart board, the demand from young teachers to prepare every presentation in PowerPoint, and the conversion of all content into modular, deliverable lessons are the new commonplaces of curriculum. In any of these exercises, the computer is not just helping the teacher, it is also considerably, radically, shaping the teacher's activity, particularly the core of that activity, which is to bring a certain degree of warmth and unpredictability through the relational aspect of teaching. The more the computer mediates, the more predictable it wants learning to become. That is the heart of the promise that the computer industry offers to education. When it focuses on outcomes of learning, that is what it exactly means—that the outcomes of this kind of learning will be more predictable and therefore, more cost-effective and justifiable. In our times, when cost-effectiveness, accountability, transparency, etc. have become values of the highest order in governance, it is not surprising that the relational aspect of teaching has lost out as a value. It is no more regarded as relevant. The meaning of individuating has also undergone a change. Computer-based teaching individuates the learner by presenting a range of choices in pacing, groping towards new items, seeking clarification, etc. These choices, however, do not include the uncertainty that makes teacher–student relationship a matter of constant negotiation.

The transformation of workplaces on account of digital machines and media is a historical reality. As worksites, educational institutions like schools and colleges too have changed over the recent years, though the extent of the change differs across countries. A digitally advanced nation like Japan has so far retained the classroom ethos in its pre-computer age character, confining digital means of information and interaction to a computer lab. This systemic resistance contrasts with the Indian response in which digitalisation has received the highest possible priority even if the physical and academic realities of schools have posed resistance. Across Europe, we can witness varying responses to the offerings that computer-related techniques and devices make to the teacher's work. Clearly, the digital conquest of school as a workplace is far from complete. At the level of higher education, the picture is only somewhat different. The propagators of online teaching have viewed higher education as a relatively more open market for the expansion of digital teaching.

Second Orbit: Knowledge

The assumption that education is mainly about knowledge has made the computer and computer-based technologies like the internet very popular and attractive in the field of education. Knowledge tends to form a body, a store, and these technologies promise to provide access to the great pile of knowledge that human beings have created over a long history of knowledge production. The access that computer technology offers to this store is fairly remarkable in terms of ease, speed and accuracy. If you have the right question and the right keywords, you can quickly get the right bit of information. The speed at which you get access to the general store of knowledge is also remarkable. The nature, range and the speed of access are very important features as far as the 'store' aspect of knowledge is concerned. The other aspect, namely knowledge creation as an essential experience of education, is also facilitated by computer-based technology. It offers us a speedy exchange of ideas, information and new findings among people who are in similar pursuits. Teachers and scholars, researchers and students can exchange ideas with each other as they pursue knowledge. These key attractions are often presented as the power of the new technology to democratise knowledge. Knowledge, which has always been a factor of social exclusion, suddenly is reported to be turning a corner. We are told that knowledge need not anymore be an exclusionary factor as we now have a technology that is going to democratise knowledge by providing free or very low-cost access to anyone and everyone, therefore, the era of social inequality and disadvantages can now be said to be behind us. What was left to do, we were told, was to prepare ourselves for a more equal world: by creating structures that will permit us to manage this new world which will be equal in terms of access to knowledge. 'Knowledge is a variable of exclusion' is no more relevant—this is what one learns from the perspective of technology. I have just listed a few of the grounds on which this is argued.

Let us look at education briefly. Education actually does not deal directly with knowledge. That has to be remembered as we go deeper into this matter. If education was directly involved with knowledge, then learning would be a very serious problem for children. Children obviously are at a disadvantage compared to somebody who is elder to them, who knows more; and not only knows more, but knows that a great deal of knowledge has already been created. That is why modern educational theory, which has entrenched itself quite firmly over the last century in the way children think or how children's minds grow, reminds us that education is not so much about knowledge as about establishing the desirability of knowledge and about gaining the means by which one can practise or fulfill this desire. These are more defensible statements about education—that when we are able to receive education at the hands of a teacher, the teacher's main job in relation to knowledge is really to establish that it is worth striving for. I think the teacher finds it challenging precisely because striving for knowledge is not all that pleasant or convenient. I realise that many slogans, such as 'joy of learning', distract us into thinking that the pursuit of knowledge is a pleasure. The teacher's job is to make knowledge desirable, something worthwhile despite the hard work it demands and the inconveniences of doing that kind of work daily. In the warmth of a pedagogic relationship, the student notices that he or she is gradually getting inducted into a community which is based on knowledge. That is a very pleasurable feeling. No matter where you come from, if you feel that you are entering a community that has existed before you and your presence and work will widen it, you will find this a deeply satisfying thought.

This is the role that education has in the context of knowledge. This role depends on the trajectory of learning from a teacher who acts as an enabler: someone who gives you a taste for learning. Gradually you discover that not all the knowledge that is there in the world needs to be learnt; that, in fact, you will access the existing stock of knowledge by creating a personal niche of meaning. This is what education has the potential to do. When the computer and the internet offer us access to the vast storehouse of knowledge at great speed, they present a kind of a proximity to sources of knowledge. This feeling is somewhat unwarranted, partly because the proximity is not all that clear. The range of our potential access to knowledge is much too vast and the necessity to exercise choice is a compulsion. The teacher's attempt to mediate between the learner and the world's stock of knowledge is disrupted or intercepted because this very powerful tool is able to make the student feel far more empowered than a teacher can. Also, a computer can make you feel empowered faster and with a greater sense of advantage.

A tussle ensues, therefore, when computer-mediated technologies define and redefine the work that a teacher does. It is not particularly clear how this new access to knowledge can sit with the teacher's role in mediating between the student and the store of knowledge that exists. The teacher's regulatory or calibrating role is significantly intercepted now by the technology which offers any amount of and any level of knowledge at a much greater speed and makes students feel free to exercise their choices in terms of either the depth or the range of access to knowledge. Teachers are a bit cornered. They are still doing their work—so long as they have work—attempting to make a relational attempt as means of establishing the desirability of knowledge. But as far as furnishing the content, in which that relationship will grow and acquire its warmth, is considered, that is no more tied to the teacher's effort to establish a relationship. A far vaster amount of content is now available to the student and the teacher as well. It is a very different kind of question as to who is creating that content. A computer, after all, is a product. It is a tool in the market and therefore what it offers is shaped by the market. A lot of content available to the student for various areas of knowledge is packaged, presented and made accessible through the filters of corporate wisdom and decision-making. The teacher is truly cornered, because teaching is a relatively humbler activity than running a corporation and, in that sense, the teacher's ability to use the content of knowledge to bring warmth into his or her relationship with the student is under great pressure. The student is no more dependent on the teacher for using the content that the teacher has chosen, nor is the student obliged to maintain the teacher's speed as his or her own speed at which the content will be encountered.

Third Orbit: Ethics

Let us now move to the third orbit, that of ethics, although, in a way, we have already moved into it. Ethics have to do with ethos; an ethos is shaped by a vast number of forces that we cannot always see and describe and therefore, the subject of how relations between education and technology may be changing the sphere of ethics can be a very complex exercise requiring a longer engagement than is possible here. Values acquire their character and meaning from the context in which they are practised. Values like commitment, loyalty or boldness, for example, are wonderful, but they completely changed meaning under Germany of the 1930s under fascist conditions. To be loyal or committed meant being committed to the mass murder of Jews. This example should suffice to say that as individual words, values can be a bit deceptive. What the value words mean always requires a consideration of the context in which we attempt to understand how those values manifest in a given period of history, under certain conditions and so on. That is a useful marker at this juncture when we are trying to engage with this very complex third orbit of ethics in the context of education and technology's relationship at a moment of tremendous technological change and the changes that technology has already brought into education as a system.

I will focus on just one value and the behaviour associated with it. That value is waiting. I will look at waiting in relation to knowledge as a necessary aspect of the pedagogic relationship between a teacher and a student, and then examine how waiting behaviour is being shaped by computer technology. As a value behaviour, waiting involves certain qualities, such as patience. If you are going to wait, you will have to have patience, and when waiting gets longer patience must turn into endurance.

If waiting is a value behaviour, then patience and endurance both must be practised without anger, because anger will spoil the value character of waiting. For waiting to be practised, patience and endurance must be viewed as worthwhile. It is important to be able to contain the anger that the exercise of patience for a long time necessarily risks; similarly, endurance for a long time does risk loss of patience, and therefore the expression of anger.

These points are highly relevant to the pursuit of knowledge. What the teacher tries in a pedagogic relationship with the student is essentially to sustain the hope in the student's mind that a time will come when things will make sense. In the meanwhile, a lot of things will have to be learnt that do not necessarily come together. Thus, maintenance of hope and sustenance of the desire to learn is something very primary to the teacher's job, because the teacher is attempting to induct the student into a community based on knowledge. The teacher is making knowledge desirable despite the pain, suffering and sacrifice it involves. It is a teacher's job to maintain hope for a long period of time. The time period may not be as long in the early stages of learning, that is, during childhood, as it might be in later stages of learning, but prolonging the pursuit and the hope of its success is necessarily a part of the teacher's job. There may be smaller fruits available on the way, but the teacher's job is to make the student wait for the bigger fruit—of understanding a problem or a theme. The teacher cultivates the ability to create the means to grapple with an issue and ensures that when the result is achieved, it does not look trivial. In fact, that is the one danger that the teacher is always trying to avoid, namely, that if some important insight is achieved too early, it may not strike the young student as an insight; he or she may take it as something rather trivial. The teacher's attempt really is to let the truth dawn on you when you can appreciate it, because you have worked so hard for it. A teacher's job becomes more difficult, sensitive and subtle precisely because of his or her attempt to make you wait and exercise patience. The teacher's role is of a regulator who is aware of the stages through which the student's learning and attempts must pass and the errors that might be made before the moment of understanding is arrived at. That is the heart of this pedagogic relationship in the context of ethics that we are talking about.

If we now compare this challenge of engagement with knowledge in the company of a teacher with what it becomes in the company of a computer, a whole lot of things attain clarity. One reason why the computer is so attractive is that it does not make us wait. In fact, any attempt on its part to make us wait makes us anxious about its age. If the internet takes a few extra moments to respond, we begin to wonder about the provider. Even a few seconds' wait can be intolerable in our times. The idea that I need not wait to find the answer or relevant information is very central to computer-mediated learning.

Computer-mediated learning means that you do not need to endure those hours, days or months when you wait to find the answer to a question. You can be enlightened very quickly on any theme or topic, and that is precisely its main attraction. The computer offers you instant gratification as opposed to the delayed or deferred gratification that the teacher trains you to appreciate. The computer makes the postponement of the moment of finding an answer fairly irrelevant. If you have a query, question or curiosity, computer technology suggests you can satisfy that curiosity quickly. Professor Yash Pal's book *Discovered Questions*, which is a collection of a vast number of questions (that children asked him over the years and he answered in various media), is an interesting book to refer to at this juncture.[2] Essentially, what this great scientist's answers are all about is that he allowed his mind to grow over a period of time. Children brought him all kinds of questions. Many were way beyond the borders of his own subject—physics—and capacities as a scholar of astrophysics and as a nuclear scientist. The questions he received were borderless. When you read this book and notice the way in which he attempts to negotiate different kinds of questions from a whole range of subjects and topics from daily life, you discover what he does. His technique consists of living with a question; in many cases, his life with a question is very obvious in the description he offers us in the answer. He suggests that when he started to live with the question, it began to attract information long buried in his mind. Sometimes, when he talked to people about the question he was living with, they reminded him of things that he thought he knew but had forgotten. At other times, he was able to make connections on his own while reading something. Eventually the question took a different form; typically, if you read this book, you will notice that the question a child had asked becomes a bigger and wider question: it brings with it so many other questions which Yash Pal gifts back to the child. In that sense he is able to act as a teacher who does not answer a question directly; instead he acts as an enabler, by permitting children to think about many more questions of that kind.

This technique necessarily depends on the point that John Holt had made in one of his early books, *How Children Fail.*[3] During his teaching, he made sure that no question was ever answered quickly. He trained children to learn to live with a question, to remember it a week later, two weeks later or as long as they can retain it. Sometimes children he taught did forget the question and Holt used to remind them what it was. That way, he was practising what Yash Pal actually practised in his role as a respondent to children's questions in the media. The idea was that when we live with questions, our insight, our interest and our engagement with knowledge also grows. This aspect of questions and sustained curiosity as a necessary part of learning is dependent on practising the value behaviour of waiting with patience and without letting curiosity die. That is how curiosity turns into inquiry. If it stays long enough, and it is permitted to grow in the crucible of our minds, then it acquires the shape of the kind of connectivity in the mind which computer-based connectivity makes irrelevant. It answers us quickly, takes us from question to question and opens our mental doors to questions that we had not thought of, or information sources that we were not aware of. It is a very different engagement with knowledge. It is certainly not based on waiting as a value. What it means in terms of the ethos it creates for educational institutions is something that ought to be studied. Computer-mediated learning is much too new today. In most of our institutions, it was not available a couple of decades ago. We do not exactly know what it does to the ethos in which we hope to practise the only work we know how to do, that is, teaching, and what our students do, that is, learning. We do not quite know how the ethics of learning are being shaped in learning through a computer or in an environment which is greatly suffused with computer technology. The ethical changes that the popularity of computer technology is bringing about are numerous. From truth to authenticity, a vast range of values are undergoing significant transformation in their social meaning. This is a major cultural phenomenon and it needs to be studied even as we feel compelled to join the chorus of enhanced space for computer technology in education.

Conclusion

The relationship between technology and education today, like many other relationships, has become a subject of a highly polarised kind of debate. The advocates of technology and its quick application in education become impatient whenever a plea is made for studying it. Any plea for better understanding or study makes them feel that they are listening to a techno-sceptic. The remarks I have made in this essay will doubtless strike a techno-romantic as those of a techno-sceptic, and this is the polarity I am referring to. The dialogue between a techno-sceptic and a techno-romantic cannot take place for an obvious reason: the techno-romantic does not want to waste his time with a sceptic. The romantic vision that promoters of technology propagate is much too attractive. It promises the transformation of the world and education. It is a compelling dream; it leaves no need to listen to a sceptic or even to study the matter. The techno-romantic point of view essentially pushes the techno-sceptic to look more and more cynical or irrelevant. If you are dealing with this subject in an academic institution, the likelihood is that you will not get very far. The technological vision is not just dominant today, with strong vested interests driving it forward, it has, in fact, already swept away much of the conceptual legacy of education as a social system.

Therefore, although it sounds a bit late in the day, we have every reason to believe that a plea for studying the relationship between education and computer technology is never too late. We need to examine how technology is affecting work, particularly the teacher's work, how it is shaping the relations between education as a social institution and work in society. We do need to inquire carefully and spend time, even if we are made to think that the matter is no more relevant as a subject of research and reflection. Education equips us to think and investigate: that is our job. We do need to study the relations between technology and knowledge, and how knowledge-based technique of access is shaping teaching. These questions need to be studied over a period of time, with the help of our students whose lives are more deeply intertwined with computers than ours might be as older teachers. We need to look at the question of knowledge in relation to teachers' lives, their services, their diverse roles in different aspects and spheres of the academia. And finally, we need to study the whole sphere of values—how technology is reshaping what we consider to be a good life. Is a good life the same as a convenient life that technology offers us? If it is, is it practised with certain exclusions that we are not aware of? Is the promise of a technology-based democracy related to the rise of a technocratic democracy?

Notes

1. Ursula Franklin, *The Real World of Technology* (Toronto: Anansi, 1993).
2. Yash Pal and Rahul Pal, *Discovered Questions* (New Delhi: NCERT, 2009).
3. John Holt, *How Children Fail* (New York: Dell, 1964).

Index